Warren Hope Dawson

Warren Hope Dawson

The Journey of an

African Legal Eagle

Sula
TOO

Sula Too Publishing
Tampa, Florida

Copyright © 2021 Warren Hope Dawson
All rights reserved. This book may not be reproduced in whole or in part without written permission from the publisher, except by a reviewer who may quote brief passages in a review; nor may any part of this book be reproduced, stored in retrieval system, or transmitted in any form or by any means, electronic, mechanical, photocopying, recording, or other, without written permission from the publisher.

ISBN-13:978-0-9791560-5-2
Library of Congress Control Number: 2020918619

Printed and bound in USA
First Printing 2021

All photographs are owned by
the author unless otherwise credited

Published by Sula Too Publishing
www.sulatoo.com/publishing

Dedication

*To My Mother, Naomi Warren Dawson,
who gave me all she had - and more; who
demanded of me all she had given - and more.
&
To each child whose formal education
for the life ahead begins at
The Warren Hope Dawson Elementary School.*

Contents

Dedication	**5**
Forward	**9**
Childhood Years	**15**
College Years	**53**
Military Years	**63**
Launching A Career	**96**
A 27 Year Battle	**124**
Legendary Fights	**135**
The Quest for Public Office	**165**
There is Always a Way	**185**
My Support System	**204**
In Conclusion	**209**

Forward

When I consider: the humble place where I started; the many stops, starts and places experienced along the way; and finally, the blessed place where I finished, I am persuaded that my life has been a journey – not a trip but a journey. Traveling from point A to point B is adequately described as a trip. Going from A to B and then to C and later to D, E, F and G is a journey. Happy at this point? Yes! Determined to continue? Yes! So, moving on to H, I, J, K, L, M and N. Blessed to have come that far? Yes! Willing to rest at that point? No! Are O, P, Q, R, S, T, U, V, W, X, Y and Z worthy of pursuit? Yes! "Journey" is the word I use because it fully captures the travels of my life: its ups and downs; its twists and turns; its wins and losses; its thrills of victory, its agonies of defeat; its surprises and its disappointments.

The lawyer I became had absolutely nothing to do with how this journey began. Stated otherwise, it didn't begin as a lawyer, it began as a gospel singer. I refer to some of the songs I sang as they have recurred to me as I journeyed through this life. That's a fact I invite you to remember.

In many ways, my middle name, HOPE, set the tone for my mission in life. Throughout my years, repeatedly I tried to bring hope to situations that appeared hopeless. Much of what I tried to do evolved from my fifty plus years in the active practice of law. In that endeavor, I strove to be a catalyst for positive change in the lives of those I served and, in the community where I lived. I set about to reject the notion that "Hope unborn" could die.

A daily newspaper once proclaimed:

"Dawson has blended a law practice with a dedicated, lifelong pursuit of racial equity and justice. Dawson (has) demonstrated backbone, tenacity, diplomacy, and courage…"

To which I say: the paper got it right!

Finally, I acknowledge that the reference to myself as an Eagle is unabashedly bold. Bold? Moi? In the view of some, that is an understatement. So, whither "African Legal Eagle?" Well, I could have simply embraced "Legal Eagle", but I was much too Afro-centric to omit a reference to the Mother Land. Now, some might inquire as to whether there are eagles in Africa? My response: Yes, "I" have been there several times. In either event, wherever they are found, they are like leaders, they don't flock. You find them one at a time. This whole "Eagle" idea has been key to my endurance in the midst of intense challenges. The image of an African Eagle helped me to stay focused, to rise above the noise and to land with the confidence of an African warrior. Thus, I have seen life through the eyes of an African Legal Eagle.

As you will come to know from my journeys included here, I have been to every quadrant of the African Continent and yet I am a little like Nikole Hannah-Jones, The 1916 Project, who acknowledged:

> *"It seemed that the closest thing black Americans could have to cultural pride was to be found in our vague connection to Africa, a place we had never been."*

As for the "Journey" highlighted by this book, I am reminded of a client whose case I successfully litigated against the Hillsborough County Sheriff's Department. After some three years of litigation, I was finally ready to close her case and to disburse to her the money I had won on her behalf. While I knew she had relocated to Baltimore, Maryland; I did not know she had, during those three years, given birth to twin boys and a separate birth to a little girl.

Unaware of her life changes, I arranged for her to make the trip from Baltimore to Tampa to receive her money. Well, she missed her flight to Tampa and took a later one to Orlando, where she rented a car and drove to Tampa. She finally arrived at my office more than four hours late. While she apologized for being tardy, she went on to tell me how much she had enjoyed her journey, particularly the drive from Orlando to Tampa during which she had the pleasure of being alone with good music on the radio. With her little ones safely in the hands of caregivers, momentarily she was free from her motherly responsibilities and enjoying every moment of her journey. She said, the closer she got to Tampa the slower she drove so as to extend the serenity of her journey. The money that awaited her at her destination was clearly secondary.

I offer this book as insight into the many stories, causes, situations, obstacles, opportunities, disappointments, privileges and joys I have encountered along this journey. In the memorable words of that gospel song:

I Won't Complain

I've had some good days
I've had some hills to climb
I've had some weary days
I've had some sleepless nights

But when I look around
And I think things over
All of my good days
Outweigh my bad days
So I won't complain

As you follow my journey, consider that it all began in Prairie, a laborer's quarters of a phosphate mining company located just north of Mulberry, Florida. This phosphate miner's son has since traveled many miles, been to a lot of places, met a lot of people, done a lot of things, fought a lot of battles, overcame a lot of disadvantages, survived and often thrived in many extraordinary situations.

A stand-out part of my journey as a lawyer is surely the twenty-seven years I spent litigating the school desegregation case known as Manning vs. the School Board of Hillsborough County, Florida. Few lawyers have spent that many years litigating a single case. Now, twenty-seven years may seem like a lifetime for some; yet, it was only a small part of my life in the law.

As I reflect on the stories emerging from my years, I suggest it would have been difficult, if not impossible, to predict how well it all turned out. Simply stated, my life has been a good life – a good life well lived, while making sure it was not all about me. Instead, it has largely been about how I could change things to benefit others using my legal talents, my fierce determination, my activism in the community and my perfected refusal to accept "no" as the answer.

As I begin this book about my life, I am reminded of the Bible verses Matthew 16:13-16, where Jesus asked his disciples *"Who do men say that I, the Son of Man, am?"* Jesus listened to their responses and then asked, *"Who do you say that I am?"* After hearing their responses, he then instructed the disciples on what he called himself. This book, in many of its parts, is about who I say that I am. I am that child that was born to a woman who had two prior miscarriages. I was determined to go to full-term and to arrive alive. With that task completed, I have been running ever since, determined to succeed. That set the pace for my life. Focused and disciplined – that would be me. Delayed, yes, but not denied – that would also be me.

Finally, as Gladys Knight sang, *"If anyone should write my life story, for whatever reason there might be,"* I offer this book as my version of what I have done and who I say that I am.

Warren H Dawson

Chapter 1

Childhood Years

Hope Began In Mulberry

What's in a Name?

It is interesting that much of my life would be devoted to resolving legal problems because, as it turned out, I had a legal problem within a few weeks after my birth. You see, at birth, my mother named me "Adam Lee" Dawson honoring the first names of her parents, Adam and Letha Warren.

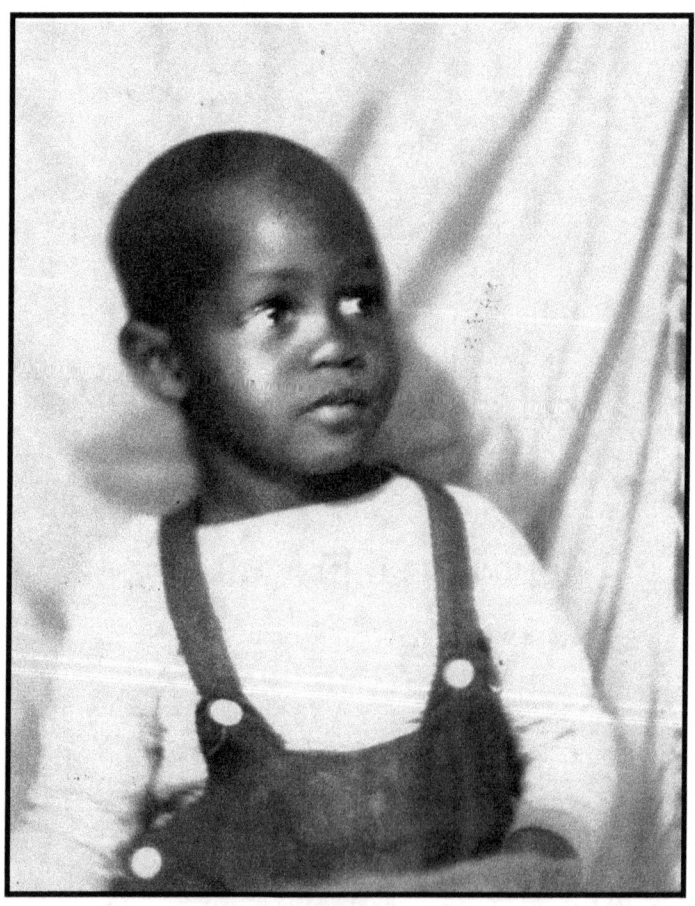

Earliest photo of Warren Hope Dawson

Several weeks later, Mother realized her mistake. She had intended to give me her parent's last or family surname, "Warren," rather than the combination of their first names. So, without making it official, she changed my name to "Warren Hope Dawson." My godmother, Vernice Williams, suggested the name "Hope," apparently related to the Opal, October's birthday birthstone, which symbolizes hope.

Some twenty eight years later, in 1967, I passed the Florida Bar Examination and the Supreme Court of Florida issued my certificate to practice law in the name of "Adam Lee Dawson." That decision of the Court presented me with the first legal problem of my career as a lawyer. It forced me to petition for a name change to reflect the name I had used all of my life, i.e. "Warren Hope Dawson."

However, to be clear I, Warren Hope Dawson, was born October 17, 1939, to Japhus Lloyd Dawson and Naomi Warren Dawson in Prairie/Mulberry, Florida, whose first legal task was to correct my real name.

As an aside, I, like most "colored" boys born in the 1930s, had a series of nicknames. For starters, my mother affectionately called me "Dee" and sometimes "Deelum." Some of my contemporaries, ostensibly my friends, called me "My-Rock," "Jazzmoe," "Dee Dawson," "Put'ng Tane", "Tampa Red," "Florida Slim," among others. On the other hand, those who were not my friends have called me such names as: the forbidden "nigger," "troublemaker," "snake," "agitator," just to name a few. At certain points in my life, I was treated as if I were a second-class citizen, an animal, a nobody, a sucker, and a slave.

I am proud to be Warren Hope Dawson - in spite of the foregoing - and I am the fellow who struggled greatly to make Warren Hope Dawson a name of honor.

> ♪ *"I tol' Jesus it would be alright if He changed my name"* ♪

Warren Hope Dawson and The Audacity of HOPE

Company Town Roots

Much about how I came to be who I became is due to my being born in Prairie, a Florida phosphate mining laborer's quarters owned by International Mineral and Chemical Company("IMC"). Prairie was located just outside of Mulberry, Polk County, Florida. Prairie was, what is known as, a "company town". Few people understand or know what a company town is or was, although several still exist. Anyone who lives in such a town knows full well what it means: The company's impact on their lives involved employment, housing, credit, and other vital aspects of everyday life. If your daddy lost his job or died, you lost everything.

My father did not lose his job. The Company took our house because they wanted to mine the phosphate under the house. They moved all laborers because the phosphate in the ground below their houses was more valuable to the company. For a nominal amount of money, you could buy the house you lived in, and the company would move it to an area named for R. B. Fuller, the company's general manager. My father declined that offer, and in 1946, he arranged to build a new house in town, in Mulberry. Unfortunately, due to bad wiring, in February of 1947, that house burned down. Early one morning, shortly after father left for work, he looked back and saw flames and smoke coming from our newly built home. He turned around, entered the house, and escorted us out by leading Mother and me across burning boards to safety.

Tragically, Father died in 1948, just as he completed

Japhus Lloyd Dawson, Sr. and Naomi Warren Dawson

rebuilding our home. At the time of his death, I was nine years old and was thereafter reared by my mother, without a father.

Prairie did yield a lifetime friend, Tommie Martin. Tommie was born in the house next door to me in Prairie. Our houses were "on The Hill." The Dawson and the Martin families were the only two black families on "The Hill" and located behind the IMC executive offices.

There was Prairie, Little Prairie and there was "The Hill". Many years later Tommie bought a house across the street from mine in Tampa, Florida.

A Brain Wired For Details

My mother, for many reasons, would often go back to her home in Darlington, South Carolina. Every time the school doors closed, we would hit the road en route to South Carolina. Sometimes returning days or even weeks after the school session had begun. At best, we would return just in the nick of time for the first day of class.

Although I am a native-born Floridian, I had the high privilege and the great agony of picking cotton, attending to farm animals, shucking corn, putting in tobacco, pulling fodder, and learning the various stages of corn transformation into table food all on my grandfather's farm in Darlington, South Carolina. We harvested our corn and took it to a mill. From the mill, we brought home sacks of corn in the form of cornmeal, other sacks as grits and yet other sacks as flour. Those products were made from corn by its various degrees of grinding. No money was exchanged; we exchanged corn for cornmeal, grits, and flour.

During my early years, we "caught the bus" to South Carolina. As a result, by the time I was eight years old, I had memorized every stop from Mulberry, Florida to Darlington, South Carolina. As a form of child's play, I would sit in a rocking chair on my grandmother's porch and "drive the bus." To my family's amazement, I could recite every stop the bus made. I called out the rest stops and announced to my imaginary passengers they could get off for a brief time. I literally knew every stop.

Since my father died when I was nine, I grew up rather quickly. By age ten, I could read a road map. That was one of my first tasks as my mother's right-hand driver-man.

Because Mother was nervous about a rickety wooden bridge in Charleston, South Carolina, called the "Cooper River Bridge," my task was to chart a course from Mulberry to Darlington avoiding that bridge at all cost. Initially, it was her desire for us to cross into South Carolina on old Highway 17 and find our way to Darlington without going through Charleston. Ultimately, I mapped out a route to pass Beaufort, then make a left turn, travel through Walterboro, Sumter and then into Darlington. As time went on, we would also drive from Darlington across South Carolina to Anderson, my father's hometown. So, I learned that part of South Carolina as well. I came to know South Carolina like the back of my hand. Yes, some small unincorporated towns may have escaped me; however, if the town was of any size, I was aware of it. I knew South Carolina better than I knew Florida.

Mother purchased a car by the time I was thirteen, and I was able to drive it because I was tall and appeared old enough to drive.

My attention to detail and willingness to take charge of a situation, when necessary, have been with me for quite some time. That skill has served me well.

I Am My Mother's Son

Mother was a musician and that fact shaped much of my life. My earliest memories are of singing and traveling with her. Doing so exposed me to a broad range of experiences, none of which I regret because they essentially became a part of my DNA.

There is a photograph I haven't seen since I was nearly fourteen years old, that bears witness to how early I began singing publicly. In that photo, I was about three years old and dressed in a cutaway tuxedo, the kind of little-boy's formal tuxedo you see in weddings. It reminded me of a picture I have seen of Sammy Davis, Jr when he was dancing with his uncle, as a part of the "Will Mastin Trio." If you find that photograph of me, please let me know.

Mother was a very popular musician functioning as a pianist, vocalist, choir director, and teacher. Today, she would be considered a minister of music. In her day, a woman generally would not refer to herself as a minister of any kind. In fact, I can only recall a few women who were pastors of a church. Pastor Rebecca Corbett, the mother of C.C. and J.J. Corbett, was pastor of Gregg Temple, A.M.E. Church. A church she founded in Bradley Junction, Florida, and named it for A.M.E. Bishop John Andrew

Gregg. The other woman preacher was the extremely good looking B. Margretta Jones from Philadelphia. My mother probably elected not to "preach", as such, but to preach through her music.

Mother was born into a family of people who belonged to African Methodist Episcopal (A.M.E.) Church in Darlington, South Carolina. She, as did I, became committed to the A.M.E. Church and loyal to family history. However, she in her mind, for herself and me as her child, believed there was a higher power with a higher degree of vision beyond the church we knew. Thus, we became involved with evangelical, Holy-Ghost-type churches. She was sanctified and holy in addition to being an A.M.E. member. She also had no problem at all with getting happy, while singing and playing, and she was in no way ashamed to show her "happiness."

Well, that may have worked for her, but for a young lad who had to deal with the reactions of his peers, Mother's episodes of getting happy and feeling the Holy Spirit became the source of considerable embarrassment to me. My peers teased me mercilessly. In some instances, they even imitated the various ways she showed her religious happiness.

That embarrassment was compounded by the then prevailing notion, among my peers, that fellows who played the piano were gay. So, with every fiber in my body, I successfully resisted my mother's efforts to teach me to play the piano, even though a piano was being played in our home nearly every hour of the day. On the other hand, I did learn to sing, and singing later became my ticket to college. In 1957, I was offered, and accepted, a choir scholarship to attend Florida A & M University and I sang in the University Concert Choir. Through it all, I did develop a good feel, appreciation and ear for music that has never gone away.

I credit Mother with my ability to speak and to speak on an impromptu basis. Without warning, she would, as the Sunday School Superintendent in our small church, call on me and say, "Dee, review the Sunday School Lesson." That review would be for the entire church, the adults, and the kids. In fact, I did enjoy the attention of the entire church. Little did I know, those early childhood speaking experiences would serve me well in my future college debates, my mock legal cases in law school, and in my future career as a trial lawyer.

Mother also handled all youth productions, for Christmas and Easter, at our little church. Of course, she made sure I had both a singing and speaking part in all productions, including the all-too-familiar child recitation:

> *Hello!*
>
> *I didn't come to stay*
> *I just came to say,*
> *Happy Easter Day*

To give a complete picture of our religious routine: our Sunday morning started with a 6:00 a.m. "morning prayer service" at home; by 9:00 a.m., we were at church for Sunday School; and at 11:00 a.m. Morning Worship Service began. After an early afternoon lunch, we would return at 3:00 p.m. for Afternoon Worship Service; and at 6:00 p.m. for Night Service. Bear in mind, those services did not adhere to a definite schedule, except for starting times. Consequently, many services would be two hours or longer, which made for some very long Sundays.

After night service, my mother refused to go home if there was any church in our little town that was still in session. When we would finally go home, quite often it was after midnight, and as late as 1:00 a.m., Monday morning. That was not just one Sunday, but every Sunday.

During the summers, we traveled extensively. I found myself sitting in many, many churches between Mulberry and New York City. We attended services all along the eastern seaboard of the United States in countless towns and hamlets. We even sang for tent revivals.

I grew up watching a lot of the preachers across all denominations, including those involved with the charismatic church. In that regard, I came to know religious characters such as "Sweet" Daddy Grace, Father Devine, Prophet Jones, Elder Michaux and others.

Mother played for Beulah Baptist Church in Swift (now Agricola), Florida for Rev. J. D. Dupree. Rev. Dupree was also the pastor for St John Baptist Church in Clearwater, Florida and the Moderator for the Union Foreign Missionary Baptist Association, INC. (which still exists). We took the trip to Swift every 2nd and 4th

Sundays. Rev. Durpree came from Tampa, stopped in Mulberry to pick us up and we rode en route to Swift.

I spent a great deal of time riding in the back seat of this man's car as we travel back and forth to Swift (Agricola). Swift was a company town nine miles southwest of Bartow, Florida that was built in 1907. It was one of those company towns mentioned earlier that was built to house employees of phosphate mining companies.

One summer, my mother accepted employment in Norfolk, Virginia at a music house. Her employer was Ms. Cordelia Monroe, a fierce entrepreneur who hailed from Chicago, Illinois. Another summer, when I was in the seventh grade, she worked for Ms. Monroe, who owned an additional music store in Baltimore, Maryland. During that stay, we sang on street corners to the beat of tambourines and drums.

My account of this time frame would not be complete without sharing more of my Baltimore experience. When I was in seventh grade, and after my father died, Ms. Monroe finally prevailed upon my mother to work for her full time. We went to Baltimore and lived at 1330 Pennsylvania Avenue. I remember the address because it was directly across the street from the Royal Theater, where all the stars came to perform. During that time, I attended School #130 on McCulloh Street in Baltimore. We lived upstairs over the music store in the roughest neighborhood in town.

Every day, I walked several blocks to school and I was beaten up almost daily. Before we made that move to Baltimore, my mother bought a trumpet for me. I had taken lessons from a man named Mr. Pope, who taught

Japhus Lloyd Dawson, Jr., Naomi Warren Dawson and Warren Hope Dawson

music at the high school in Lakeland, Florida.

One day in Baltimore, I was walking to school and a gang of four or five guys jumped on me, hit me with a chain, and took my trumpet. The physical and emotional pain was unforgettable. I never got another trumpet.

Also during that time frame someone, who was my mother's age and friend, shared with me a secret pleasure of adult life. To say the least, the Baltimore experience was truly a "coming of age" event for me. Even at my tender age, it was clear to me that we had to get out of Baltimore and get back home to little Mulberry to save my body and my soul.

The call back to Mulberry was ever present. We were constantly reminded of Mulberry by the "telephone exchanges." MU was an exchange prefix for some telephone numbers, and it was short for Mulberry; therefore, we would often see something like MU 774774. In Baltimore, many of the taxi cabs would have Mulberry spelled out, and their advertisement would beckon you to call Mulberry 774774.

As for Mother, Baltimore was where she showcased her talents. She was one of a very limited number of gospel musicians in the 1940s and 50s who could read music. God also blessed her with the talent to sight-read music. She could take a piece of sheet music she had never seen before, put it on the piano and play it through about 80% correct on the first attempt. That's why the music store owner hired Mother and convinced her to relocate to Baltimore.

My mother, Naomi Warren Dawson

My singing career started at age three, and continued until I was around fourteen or fifteen. That is when I self-emancipated from singing gospel music with my mother. And of course, that did not make her happy.

Interestingly, favorable respect was given by my peers to those who sang secular music. So, I stepped up my imitations of Nat King Cole, Billy Eckstine, and similar artists. That invariably meant I would be called upon, which I didn't mind, to sing in secular situations.

One of the most memorable occasions was singing for the dedication of the newly built Union Academy High School in Bartow, Florida. At the time, I was in the eleventh grade. Somewhere along the way, it was rumored that I had not completely learned the words to the song "Bless This House." That is when I received a telephone call from my high school principal, Mr. James Stephens.

Mr. Stephens said, "Mac (he called all guys Mac), I understand you do not know the words to the song you are scheduled to sing." I said; "Oh yeah Mr. Stephens, I know the words." He then said, "Okay Mac, sing it to me right now over the telephone. Go ahead, sing it." Of course, I couldn't. I didn't know all the words. He basically said he would have my hide if I didn't learn them and learn them quickly.

Needless to say, I was not going to risk public embarrassment and another encounter with Mr. Stephens, so I learned the song. I will share more about Mr. Stephens later.

Since that kind of singing carried no peer stigma, I began singing more and more Nat King Cole style music. Of course, that did not please my mother; however, by that point in my life, the love of music had become deeply ingrained. After all, I was my mother's son.

Then, in 1983, it was time to say goodbye. My mother died.

By that time black people, in my part of the world, were no longer having funerals on Sundays. The black preachers had put a halt to that practice. From their perspective, Sunday funerals were taking money out of their pockets. While Sunday was indeed the Lord's Day, it was also the preacher's day – to be paid. However, in 1983, when my mother died and out of respect for the fact she had played and sang for umpteen Sunday funerals, I decided to have her funeral on a Sunday. To that idea, everyone protested – including preachers, grave diggers, etc. Nevertheless, as with so many things in this world, money-in-hand solved the problem. I just told them to tell me what was it going to cost and I would pay. The funeral was on Sunday, May 29, 1983.

Speaking of an unusual time for a funeral, I also recall the time of my father's funeral as unusual – his was a night time funeral. I was told it allowed for a convenient connection with the 11:00 p.m. train that bore his body from Lakeland, Florida to Anderson, South Carolina, for burial.

However, as I close this chapter and remember the day my mother closed her eyes here on earth, I recall the words of the song "My Mother's Eyes":

> *One bright and guiding light,*
> *That taught me wrong from right,*
> *I found in my mother's eyes.*
>
> *That road all paved in gold.*
> *Just like a wandering sparrow,*
> *One lonely soul.*
> *I walked the straight and narrow,*
> *To reach my goal.*
>
> *God's gift sent from above,*
> *A real unselfish love,*
> *I found in my mother's eyes.*

My Father and His Siblings

♪ *"Sometimes I feel like a motherless child a long way from home"* ♪

Standing L to R: Minnie Dawson Green, Ella Dawson Starks, Pearl Dawson Starks & Bud Dawson. Sitting L to R: Rossie Dawson Harrison, Japhus Lloyd Dawson, & Jannie Dawson.

My father was Japhus "Lloyd" Dawson, and his father was Lawrence Dawson. Lawrence Dawson died before I was born. However, I have seen a picture of him. I am told my Grandmother Clara, Lloyd's mother had a colorful history, moved to Oklahoma, might have remarried and had another family. Shown above is a picture of my father and his siblings which was taken circa 1925.

I did get to know both of my mother's parents, and

it is for them I am named. My mother's father was Adam Warren, and her mother was Letha Scott Warren. I have great memories of Letha and Adam Warren. The older I get, the more I think I look like Adam. He was a great man and an entrepreneur farmer. He bought what had been an entire slave plantation in rural Darlington, South Carolina. He also had houses he owned and rented out with many of his tenants being white. Mind you, this was in the 1910's, 1920's, and 1930's. He also had a large working farm with several tenants who were white. Some portions of his land were as far as the eye could see.

Although in his later years he was crippled, it did not stop Adam from working his farm. One of the life-lessons learned from him occurred when he would send me to get water from the water-pump. The water pump had a can next to it to be used to "prime the pump." The lesson was: once you get the water flowing, the very first thing that should be done is refill the can. This should be done before you get water for yourself, so if the flow fails you can prime the pump the next time you need water.

Letha Warren was totally dedicated to Adam Warren. Letha enforced or policed the rules of Adam. As the family provider, Granddaddy was offered the first and the last of everything in the house, especially during meals. You better not take the last piece of chicken, until it was first offered to Granddaddy.

Adam did not ever want Letha to leave him, not even to go on an outing with my mother during those long anticipated visits from Florida that were special occasions for both women.

Men with Broad Shoulders

There are a few men who played major roles in shaping Warren Hope Dawson and before I leave my childhood memories, I want to honor them. I firmly believe a boy child should have the benefit of male influence somewhere early in his life. A boy needs a man, or some men, as distinguished from his mother or other women in his life. I'm reminded I had the benefit of a father in the home from birth to his death. I was nine, and my father had a profound impact on all of my first nine years.

Because my father died very early in my life, I didn't get to know him as I would have liked. However, that which I did know caused me to truly love him. One of my fondest memories of him was at age six driving to Anderson, South Carolina from Mulberry, Florida in his Ford Coup.

My father was a man's man and, from the mind of a nine-year-old, a great storyteller. I was fascinated with how he could amuse other men with his stories.

He was also some 20 years older than my mother. He had been previously married with two children, James Raymond Dawson and Margaret Dawson (Hurst). It may have been some combination of their age difference, my father's prior marital experience to their mother, and this being Mother's first marriage that was the source of some problems. Father had a problem accepting my brother Japhus Jr., as his child. His rejection was so strong, my mother thought it best to place her son with her mother and father in Darlington, South Carolina.

One outstanding fact about my father was, in contrast to my mother who chastised me every day in a very convincing way, my father only spanked me once when I was seven. He may have chastised me orally other times. If so, they failed to have the impact of this specific event. On that particular day, he called me, and I ignored him and kept playing. Eventually, when I did go to him, he impressed upon me he was not happy I had ignored him. He spanked me that one and only time.

As I mentioned earlier, Father had a night-time funeral. I now speculate the intent was to bury him in his hometown, Anderson, South Carolina. The train from Lakeland, Florida that would take the casket to South Carolina left at 11:00 p.m. Thus, my guess is for purposes of the funeral home's efficiency, they preferred timing that would render this a continuous event. The funeral was at night, and we went directly from the church to the train. We boarded the train, and the coffin was loaded on the train and taken to South Carolina where he was buried. That was my father, Japhus Lloyd Dawson, Sr.

When a person dies, the truth is either buried with them, or it's revealed. When my father died, the true reason for my mother going to her hometown so often was revealed. She took every chance she could to see and help raise her son, Japhus Lloyd Dawson, Jr., my brother. He was in Darlington because my father had rejected him.

My mother brought Japhus Jr., her first born, home to Mulberry to live with us very shortly after my father's death.

One final thought regarding the placement of Japhus, Jr. in Darlington, South Carolina. Inspite of my mother's best efforts to parent at a distance, this placement didn't turn out well for my brother. My grandparents were old, and my aunt, who lived with my grandparents, had never had a child. Unfortunately, by the time he was twelve years old he was sent away to a "reform school" just outside of Columbia, South Carolina. That facility was somewhat like the notorious Dozier Reform School in Florida.

"Some of Mulberry's Colored Boys of 1939":
Elmer "Minnow" Franklin, Julious "Goat" Drayton, Warren "Dee" Dawson, Eugene "June Doc" Wesley, & Arthur "Art" White - Not shown are Willie Lawrence "Curt" Simmons, Walter Henry "Toot" Bryant, and Albert Tillman. We were all born the same year and remained friends for life.

Having no father after age nine, other men served as my role models in some rather profound ways. I grew up next door to a family with ten children. Two of them were guys essentially my age. They were Elmer Franklin and

Eugene Wesley, Jr.

Our houses were adjacent, extremely close to each other, and I spent a lot of time with the Wesleys. I was at their home almost as much as I was at mine. Since I was raised, essentially as an only child, and there were ten kids right next door to me, I could not have asked for better neighbors. The good and bad things I learned, at an early age, I am sure Elmer and Eugene Wesley played a part. We played together; we fought together; we went to school together; we shot marbles together, and we ran from the same bully together. The bully was a 200-pound kid we referred to as "Big Ten."

I might add, in a small way, Mr. Gene also vicariously acted a bit like a surrogate father. He would say, "If you don't stop that boy, I'm going to whup you." If he wanted to "whup" me, he could have.

Another friend from this time-frame was Roosevelt Smith who was two years older. He frequently demonstrated that he was the toughest and strongest guy in our age group. Years later, he traveled with me to North Carolina from Florida to be the best man in my wedding.

As the years passed, my mother began to take company with a man. I was never able to get the name of one of the first men she saw. I do recall he and my mother were in her bedroom and the door was not fully closed. As an eleven-year-old, I was offended and concerned with what he was doing in my house and with my mother.

I went into the bathroom and pulled the rifle down from above the shelf where my father had left it. My half-brother, who was in the navy, had given the gun to my father as a gift. My father kept this military rifle as a souvenir.

I went back to the door, lowered the gun and pointed it at this man through the slight opening in the door. I held it there for a while, raised it, lowered it, and then put it back on the shelf. I did not attempt to fire it, and he did not see me. I had no idea if the gun would fire if I had pulled the trigger. I did not know his name, and he did not know how close he came to meeting his demise. He never knew how close I came to getting into some serious trouble: or how a young eleven-year-old male felt about another male presenting himself as the object of his mother's eye.

This dovetails with what I think I came to know later in life about how male children are particularly protective of their mothers as contrasted with what a female child will do.

"Life is worth living because there is enough love around to keep us happy. There is love among many individuals such as sister to sister, brother to brother, mother to father, cousin to cousin and friend to friend. From my perspective, chief among all love is that of mother for her son or a son for his mother." There is no greater love than that. While it is believed that "A man's best friend is his dog, it is undeniable that a little boy's best friend is his mama."

In any event, not long after that, my mother struck up a relationship with a man on a steady basis. Even though he did not live in the house with us, he came and went every day. He also took some of his meals at home with us. The reference is to: Mr. Bubba Carter. Apparently, my mother liked him, and we spent some time together. He helped my mother financially. As I matured, I thought of him in the context of the song which says, "Color him Father." I would wrestle with him, and he would let me win. It was the kind of horseplay common between a father and son. Mr. Bubba Carter, ummm - I would color him Father.

There was a noticeable absence of male role models as teachers in schools. For my first six years of school, all my teachers were females. "Fessor" E. W. Murray came into my life for seventh and ninth grades.

"Fessor" Murray, unfortunately, suffered from alcoholism. He had been a principal at Roosevelt High School in West Palm Beach, Florida and Washington Park High School in Lakeland, Florida. Later, he came to Mulberry as principal of the J.R.E. Lee Junior High School. This Mulberry assignment was essentially a demotion for him.

He lived in one room in a house next door to mine owned by Miss Precious. "Fessor" Murray was captured by the alcohol thing. I can only recall Fessor Murray having one navy suit, and he wore it every day - to the point the suit was shiny. From about twelve noon to 1:00 p.m., he made a daily trip from the school to a nearby house where liquor was sold. Like a baseball manager walking to the mound to relieve a pitcher, he would make that daily jaunt to get that hit. It wasn't something he wanted, from all appearances, it was something he needed. Even as young children, we knew exactly what was happening.

Regardless of his vice, Fessor Murray was still quite a man who could act, sing, recite, teach and discipline in such a way you would remember. The best of his qualities showed up in his son, who became a prominent minister in the A.M.E. Church and pastor of First A.M.E. in West Los Angeles, California.

Mr. Murray was followed by a good man named Frank Conoly. Mr. Conoly was quite a hands-on guy who was an excellent English teacher specializing in diagramming sentences. He taught English to 7th through 9th graders. He also coached basketball. He was the kind of he-man-type young rebellious whipper snappers needed. Indeed, he had several occasions to use it on me. Given the times, there was no legal issue with corporal punishment – and Conoly had no hesitation about laying on the leather. Teachers would beat you not only for misbehavior, but also for not "getting your lesson." As early as third grade, if Mrs. Altamese Hinson detected you were putting a wrong answer on the blackboard, she would hit you across the back that would slam you into the blackboard. She would later endear herself by preparing the best "pigs-in-the-blanket" to help raise needed funds for the school.

I remember a time when I attempted to defy Mr. Conoly. He had put out the word he didn't want any of his students sitting on a bench in front of a small grocery store very near to the school grounds. Most students, including me, abided his order, except one day at about 3:31 p.m., I decided to challenge his standing order. In my mind, He was no longer in a position to tell me what to do. After all, school was out, I was on my own time and could sit there all I wanted. So, I sat on the bench.

Someone told Mr. Conoly, he came to where I was, told me to get off the bench and go home. My position was, school was out, and he had nothing to do with where I sat. Unfortunately, he was not persuaded, and he then proceeded to get physical with me. I went home and told my mother, who then took me back to the store and told Mr. Conoly to beat me some more.

Mr. Conoly had a back-up in the 7th and 8th grades, in the person of Mr. Malvis Simmons. He was his second in command. Mr. Simmons was quite an athletic guy who had gone to Bethune-Cookman College and served in the Navy. He was a snazzy dresser and was a man with a no-nonsense approach.

It was so funny because he had a nephew who was my classmate, Willie Lawrence (Sonny) Simmons, his brother's son. He set an example of - actually "picked on"- Sonny by calling on him often to make sure he had studied and done his homework. That sent a clear message to us that we would receive the same treatment if we failed to complete our class assignments.

True to my nature, I always found a way to get involved. Even though I was not an athlete, I still found ways to get involved with athletic activities. For example, I couldn't play at any position in softball – so I worked my way into announcing the softball games on the public-address system.

At an intramural game in Fort Meade, a little microphone provided me with a golden opportunity to horn my announcing skills. I was announcing the game and said: "There is a hit by a Fort Meade player to right field and he is rounding third and coming home - where Sammy is waiting at the home plate with a roll of toilet paper to wipe him clean." Hearing this, Mr. Simmons turned around with unmistakable emotion that told me to "Bring your ass down from up there." It sent him into a rage, and my ingenious toilet paper description was my last as a beginner announcer for softball at the junior high level. However, later in college, I became the announcer for the world-class Florida A&M Marching Band.

I distinctly remember this next story because it happened during my transition from junior high to high school. During that time blacks were treated poorly, especially black men; we were at the low-end of the totem pole.

So, on this Saturday afternoon, some friends and I decided to head for Bartow to hang out at the new swimming pool, adjacent to the high school I would soon be attending.

Before I get further into the story, I need to introduce you to a central player in this story. Mr. Bill Mark, a Polk County Florida Deputy Sheriff. Bill Mark, as he was known on the street had a very well-known reputation of being very abusive to black people, specifically black men. The mere mention of his name would cause many black men to tremble in their boots – and some to urinate in their pants.

Bill Mark was the lead character in a tale involving push button windows, then a brand-new auto accessory. Reportedly, Bill Mark pulled up to a corner and beckoned this black man to come up to his car where he commanded the man stick his head in the window. Whereupon, Mark pushed the button, and the window raised up trapping the man's head in the window. Mark then yelled to the man "Boy, do you like my wife?" The man, of course, said, "No, Mr. Mark, I don't like your wife." Mark then struck him several times with a blackjack and said, "Boy, what do you have against my wife?" After striking the man several more times with a blackjack, Mark again yelled: "Boy, do you like me wife." The man then said, "Yes sir, I like your wife." Mark then struck the man many more times while asking him, "So, you like my wife huh?" Clearly, this poor black man was damned if he did and damned if he didn't.

Getting back to the story; after a fun-filled afternoon of swimming and fun, my friends and I headed to downtown Bartow to catch a ride back to Mulberry. As we came along an area, we discovered a horrible scene. We noticed Bill Mark had one hand resting on a tree with the other hand over an apparent wound to his inner thigh. Next, we saw a horrible image of Mr. Mike, the father of our friend and classmate, Lottie, laying splattered on the ground from an obvious gunshot wound.

From the smell of gun powder, the stink of blood and flesh, we knew this tragic incident had taken place only moments before we arrived. The account of events prior to the shooting was Bill Mark and his adult son, who was home visiting from college during the Christmas break, happened to encounter Mr. Mike while they were riding around in Bill Mark's unmarked police cruiser.

Mr. Mike was a rather small man, while Bill Mark was a quite large fellow. Bill Mark yelled to Mr. Mike, "Hey boy come here, where are you going?" By then, Bill Mark had gotten out of his cruiser and was walking towards Mr. Mike. Fearing the worst, Mr. Mike instantly became frightened and acted defensively and pulled out his 22. Caliber pistol and shot Bill Mark in the inner thigh.

Bill Mark's son then retrieved a very large rifle from the cruiser and shot Mr. Mike at point blank range. During the time frame of these events (circa 1953), there was no private or governmental emergency medical service (EMS) to transport injured people to a hospital. The only such service available was offered by a local funeral home, and their hearse was the ambulance.

The white funeral home dispatched its hearse to the scene. When it arrived, Bill Mark, still standing and leaning against a tree, opened the door and sat down in the front passenger seat. The hearse then pulled away leaving this critically injured black man to die right there on the ground in front of our young eyes.

How could this have been right? Why would they just leave him there to die? No one deserved this kind of treatment. But as I said earlier, "It was the times we lived in." Survival depending on your ability to endure extensive and raw racial discrimination against black people. It was part of my life while growing up in the 40s and continued throughout the 50s, 60s and beyond. To be blunt, I feared that someday I might become the next Mr. Mike unless I prepared myself to fight the evil of white privilege with my brain - not with a gun.

By this time, I was also trying to get away from spiritual music, and I would imitate Billy Eckstine and Nat King Cole. I had a pretty good imitation of those guys, and I was also moving on to high school. Principal Mr. James Stephens, who I mentioned earlier, was my principal at Union Academy High School, Bartow, Florida. Mr. Stephens, by the students, was viewed as a mythical character.

Consequently, it would take forever to talk about him except, to briefly describe him as a man of reasonably large bones, not fat, but a pretty solid guy. He had a medium brown complexion, gray eyes and two eye-teeth about one centimeter longer than you would find in most men. His teeth were the inspiration for his nickname, i.e. "wolf man." Wolf Man was commonly used by students in our conversations about him, but we would not dare use it in his presence.

The Wolf Man was principal of Union Academy School for easily thirty-five years or more. He was known for getting in your face, or on your butt, and he didn't give a damn about what year you graduated from, or quit, high school. You could have graduated one or four years ago, but upon seeing you misbehave on the street, he would discipline you right then and there. Furthermore, the Wolf Man seemed to be everywhere.

My interaction with him began when Union Academy High School was newly built. As I mentioned before he mandated I had "better not forget the words" to the song I was assigned to sing at the dedication. The music teacher had given me the responsibility of singing "Bless this House." He called me and when I told him I knew the song he replied, "Mac, well God damn it, sing it to me right now." That was his nature.

Mr. Stephens and I also shared a vice. I had cultivated a strong desire to smoke cigarettes, which was a gift from my brother, Japhus Dawson, who had finally come home to Mulberry, Florida to live with Mother and me. As early as eleven or twelve years old when I visited my grandparents in South Carolina, I would often smoke what we called "rabbit tobacco." We would roll it and smoke it as people did in South Carolina. Clearly, by the time I was in tenth grade I was a full-blown smoker with a serious smoking habit. To compound the problem, I was also Mr. Stephens' driver. I would take his car and deliver anything destined for the bank or the district office. I was chosen to make these deliveries in his car because I had a license and was a pretty good driver. Therefore, I could get away from the campus and smoke. My smoke odor could not be detected because Mr. Stephens smoked like a chimney, all anyone had to do was get into his car, and they would smell like smoke.

Childhood Ends

I attended J.R.E. Lee Junior High School from first through ninth grade. It all took place in six rooms of a building. John Robert Edward Lee, civic leader, teacher, educational-association founder, was born a slave in Texas. Lee pursued formal education, was a college teacher and administrator at several universities. He is best known for his twenty-year tenure as president at Florida A&M University.

J.R.E. Lee Junior High School

After completing J.R.E Lee as the salutatorian of my class, I was bused to Bartow to a consolidated high school for black kids called Union Academy High School. Union Academy drew kids from Mulberry, Bartow, Brewster, Bradley Junction, Agricola, Gordonville, Fullers Heights, Nichols, Homeland, and Fort Meade. Those were little phosphate industry towns serving various phosphate mining companies.

My caring and wonderful teachers at JRE LEE were: Gertrude Bentley Niece, Nell Thomas, Altamease Hinson, Dorothy Johnson, Edward Murray, Malvis Simmons and Frank Conoly.

Job Showdown - Reality Sets In

In June of 1957, I graduated from Union Academy High School in Bartow, Florida on a Friday night and left my childhood behind, although at the time, "21 was still the age of majority."

My caring and wonderful teachers at Union Academy High School were: Jeanette North, Percy Lovelace Blow, Ms. Whatley, Zelma Johnson, Alfonso Green, Forest McKinnley, Rosalyn Sippio and James Stephens.

The Monday morning following my graduation from high school, I packed a lunch box and went to work, as did most of the other young men in the area, for a phosphate mining company. I was hired by International Mineral and Chemical Corporation (IMC), the largest of several local phosphate companies operating in western Polk and eastern Hillsborough counties.

At this point, I had no serious plans for college. That is, not until an on-the-job game-changing event occurred. I got into a situation with a white man who attacked me. I was working on a drag line called "Tillie The Toiler."

It was common practice to give drag lines names, in much the same way as names are given to ships. IMC's largest drag line was "The Bigger Digger." That drag line crane, with its huge bucket, was large enough for my father to drive two automobiles into the bucket and parked them side by side. The crane was used to dig and remove phosphate rock from the ground. The rock was later processed to produce minerals, fertilizer and other crop protection products.

On the day of the big incident, I was a part of a three-man crew working "Tillie." It was a typical rainy summer Florida afternoon, in the middle of August. The crew consisted of an operator, an oiler and a grounds-man (that would be me). Each of us had assigned workstations, which were: 1) the "operator" was in an enclosed cabin about one hundred feet above the ground; 2) the "oiler" was on the second level and 3) I worked on the ground level, one hundred feet below the operator of this giant machine.

During a heavy rain storm that included a good dose of lightning, suddenly one of the major drag line cables broke. The operator stepped outside on the veranda located outside his operating cabin and yelled three stories down to me. Although I had perfect hearing at the time, I simply could not hear what he was saying. On the other hand, he was simply convinced I could hear him.

I yelled up to him, "What you say?" He replied, "Wa - Wa – Wa!!" Still not understanding him, I again screamed, "What you say?" To no avail, he again screamed in a muffled voice impossible to understand, "Wa - Wa – Wa!!"

After several more times of those exchanges, the operator concluded I was "sassing" him. I believe he then said something like: "Nigga, you know you can hear me!" Whereupon he went back into his operator's cabin, retrieved a coca cola bottle and threw it down at me. At age 18, I saw this as an act of war. So, I took my time, nearly twenty minutes, and made my way up to his operating cabin. Once there, I snatched the door open and pushed him against the wall. In short order, every available deputy sheriff in Polk County, Florida was en route to the rural location of "Tillie the Toiler."

I should comment here: my father, Japhus Lloyd Dawson, held the only long-distance trucker and chauffeur position with IMC. Dad's position was, in fact, superior to some of the jobs exclusively reserved for whites. As I mentioned previously, my father drove two autos into the bucket of a drag line to demonstrate the hugeness of this machine. He was chosen for this task because he was the number one driver for the company, one of IMC's favorite black workers, and the part-time chauffeur for R. B. Fuller, the IMC general manager. Lloyd Dawson was highly respected and very popular with everyone in the company. But by then, I was eighteen, and my dad had been dead for about nine years.

While I was not arrested, I was summarily fired and told I should never set foot on IMC's property again.

The decision to exclude me from future employment was hurtful. At eighteen, I was fatherless and jobless.

Lesson learned? It was exceedingly clear to me I was not cut out to be submissive to someone with positional authority and white privilege. For the first time, attending college became a serious option. It would probably facilitate my escape from corporate servitude and promote the "Hope" my folks had in mind when they named me.

Therefore, after the worksite confrontation, I was determined to get into college. I succeeded. I enrolled in Florida Agricultural and Mechanical University (FAMU) in Tallahassee.

Although not known at the time, Jeanette Wesley, one of the girls next door, became pregnant and gave birth to a son, Kenneth Borders. This occurred just prior to my high school graduation. In later years, it became clear to me and to others that Kenneth was my son. Jeanette's sister, Ruby, had a life-long influence over me.›

Chapter 2

College Years

A Firm Foundation

Florida A&M University

At Florida Agricultural and Mechanical University (FAMU), I emerged as a student leader and worked my way into being on the college "A" list. Initially, I received a stipend for singing in the concert choir. This financial assistance solidified my decision to go to college. Once there, I auditioned for and was chosen as "The Voice of the Marching Hundred," the famous marching band at FAMU. For introducing the band, I received another monthly check. For singing in little groups playing gigs at the then all-white Florida State University, I could earn some money. By my junior year, I entered advanced Army ROTC and became eligible for a significant monthly check from Uncle Sam. Finally, I became the lead speaker on the university's varsity debating team – for which I was also compensated. By putting all of this together, I financed my college education.

In the minds of some, there are three reasons to go to college. To learn, to grow up and to have fun. College often is the first real independent experience away from home. Of course, your parents want you to learn, and you want to have fun. Hopefully, you grow up, learn and have fun in the process. I am convinced one of the best times in your life, are your college days. Among other things, you have no money – but no debt. No one expects you to have any money and the people around you don't have any money either. College days, what a wonderful time to be alive.

Preceding the Freedom Rides, in 1958 during my sophomore year, I was returning to FAMU in Tallahassee from Mulberry by bus. From Mulberry, I had to catch a Trailways bus for the ten mile trip to Lakeland. It was virtually a city bus run for many of the black women who worked as maids and did other similar work in Lakeland.

I gave my ticket to the driver, climbed up onto the bus and sat in front in the very first seat. The driver continued what he was doing and did not see where I had chosen to sit. Finally, when he finished, he took one step up on the bus and saw me sitting in that first seat. To my surprise, he said nothing at all. Instead, he stepped back off the bus and just stood there. He stood there. And he stood there. He stood there so long, about fifteen black women in the back of the bus who had known me since I was a child, finally sensed why the bus was still sitting there and not making its way to Lakeland. It also became clear to them that this white bus driver was not going to move the bus while I was still sitting in that front seat.

The scene reminds me of the movie "The Maid." These black women, most of whom were friends of my mother, started a firestorm of demands directed to me, saying, "Boy, I don't know what you trying to do. We got to get to work. I don't know who you think you are, but we got to get to work. I know Miss Dawson would not approve of what you are doing. You need to bring your behind back here where you belong. You done gone up there to college and now you doing this."

These black women, with no help from anyone else, pressured me into moving to the back of the bus. When I did move, the driver, who had not said a word, got on the bus and we were on our way to Lakeland – of course, these nice ladies were finally on their way to work.

As ROTC partially funded my college education, there were certain requirements I had to meet, some of which were also during the summer. The summer before a ROTC officer candidate graduates from college, they attend ROTC Summer Camp. This is a cadet's intense preparation for becoming a military officer. I attended such a summer camp during the summer of 1960, at Fort Benning, Georgia. I entered summer camp as a Distinguished Military Student (DMS) and as the heir apparent to the top cadet position (Cadet Colonel) for my senior year.

Up until this point, my life had been totally segregated along racial lines. Schools, restaurants, and all other public accommodations were racially segregated. Therefore, my first experience of close social interaction with white people was at this ROTC summer camp. That was the first time in my life I had ever sat down with, had a meal with, showered in the same facility, slept in the same room, and competed academically with white people.

Weekdays, we worked day and night. Freedom came at 1:00 p.m., on Saturdays. We were allowed to leave the army base from Saturday afternoon until we had to report for our assigned duties on Monday morning.

Tuskegee Institute, now University, was only about a one-and-a-half-hour drive from Fort Benning and was a popular weekend destination. On one ill-fated Saturday afternoon, Horace Nelson a fellow FAMU ROTC cadet, and I headed to Tuskegee, Alabama to see the girls.

It was an easy cruise, and we were riding in style. Horace's mother was a high school principal from Savannah, Georgia, and apparently a woman of means. In 1958 as a sophomore, Horace had a 1958 Ford Edsel that was a gift from his mother. The Edsel was only made for a couple of years, and very few people ever owned one. In fact, Horace's car was the only one I ever saw, and I don't know of anyone else who had one. In September 1959, his mother bought him a brand-new Ford Thunderbird. We were in the Thunderbird.

After a fun-filled couple of days in Tuskegee, on Sunday evening we headed back to Fort Benning. As per usual, when I am not driving, I took a nap. A short time after we departed and while still in the famous Macon County, Alabama, I was awakened by my body being tossed around inside the car. Nelson, who had been speeding, had attracted an Alabama highway patrolman. In his own mind, Nelson decided he could out run the patrolman. To get away, he attempted to make a sharp turn onto a side road. The effort failed, and we came to an abrupt stop.

Very quickly, the patrolman was upon us and as he approached our car, his body shaking with punitive excitement. He kept repeating words we heard but couldn't understand. Much closer to us, it became clear he was saying:

"I wasn't worried about ya!" "I just wasn't worried about ya!" Then he explained. "I already called ahead and told them to pull a semi-truck across the road. So, you wasn't gonna get away. You would've barreled your ass right into that truck! I just wasn't worried about ya!"

I was twenty years old and unafraid, but it was a hellova thought: running into a semi-truck and probable decapitation.

♪ *"Nobody know the trouble I've seen-*
Well, no, nobody knows but Jesus" ♪

The patrolman then ordered Horace out of the car and locked him in the back of his cruiser. The man riding with the patrolman came and sat in Horace's car. Hollywood could not have cast a more stereotypical character. This fellow was a three hundred and fifty pound, cigar chewing, white civilian who clearly was not the local president of the ACLU. He snatched open the driver's door of Horace's new Ford Thunderbird with the intent of following the patrolman and Horace to the Macon County Jail. But there was a problem, he could not get the car started. A unique convenience feature about the 1959 Thunderbird gave him considerable trouble, the collapsible steering column.

When you put the car in park, you could move the steering wheel all the way to the right. The drive shaft moved out of place so the driver could comfortably get out of the car. It locked in place for safety. Another safety feature was the car would not crank while the steering wheel was out of its proper driving position. The man kept trying to crank the car, to no avail. Finally, out of total frustration, he took his huge arm with fat hanging down and slapped me across the chest and screamed, "How ya crank this car, boy?" At which time, I took my finger and pushed the steering column back into its locked position. Then the engine roared.

At the Macon County Jail, they put Horace in lock-up and allowed me to remain in the lobby out front. After about thirty minutes, they brought Horace back out front and allowed him to make a phone call. Of course, he called his mother who asked how much money was needed to get him out of jail. When Horace turned and asked the same question of the officer, the officer replied, "Boy, you tell her to send as much as she can send." No amount was quoted. About an hour later a western union telegram arrived, and Horace and I were finally on our way back to Fort Benning, Georgia.

Earlier I spoke to the merit of male role models during my childhood days; there is an additional key person to my development during my ROTC experience.

Captain Willie Tyus, then an Associate Professor of Military Science and Tactics at FAMU, was another significant male figure in my life. He was directly involved with the cadets, and I believe he picked who would be promoted and to which rank. He taught many of the courses we took and I, under his tutelage, became a Distinguished Military Student (DMS). He was a very straight-laced guy, small in stature and no nonsense.

I believe I caught his attention with my impressive sense of gab, my tall stature and military bearing, my academic performance, and my distinctive command voice. Unfortunately, I did not impress him with my performance during the 1960 ROTC Summer Camp at Fort Benning, Georgia. I didn't score well on some of the tests, and it was the first time I realized I might have a problem getting quality sleep at night.

Summer camp was different from regular college day-to-day. It had control of my body and my mind for twenty four hours each day. Whereas, back on the college campus, I could study, get my lesson and make good grades on my military tests. During summer camp, we would be out running maneuvers until midnight; up at the crack of dawn; in class all day; and running behind tanks all afternoon. The combination, of not having any personal time and not getting enough sleep, meant my test scores took a hit. They truly were not what they should have been. This was tough. I survived but lost the opportunity to finish as a Distinguished Military Graduate and enter as an officer in the Regular Army.

In June of 1961, the time of my graduation from FAMU, I was dating a lovely young lady named Betty Fluker from St. Petersburg. She was my girl. She also graduated that day and received a nursing degree. I went across the stage with my robe on and received my Bachelor's Degree in political science. Then I took off my robe revealing my military uniform and went back across the stage to get my commission as an officer in the United States Army Reserve.

When I came off the stage, with my shiny new gold bars, I had Betty pin them on my shoulder. Whereupon my mother promptly had an unmitigated fit, and we took the bars off so my mother could pin them on. Without question, she had fully earned the right to do so, and she was fully determined to assert her right. Of course, Mother was always right. Except for her motherly advice that I should be careful and not be caught gambling in the barracks, like the son of one of her close friends. When I told her that as an officer I would not be living in the barracks, and if anyone was gambling there it would be my duty to punish them for doing so. To which she said: "Boy, you just do what I told you."

My ROTC classmates, newly commissioned officers in the U S Army were: Remus Allen, Willie Black, Albert Brooks, Alexander Brown, Charles Buggs, Clinton Butler, Robert Catchings, Warren Hope Dawson, Tyrone Fletcher, Alvin Fridie, Emery Hamilton, Joseph Harris, Jimmie Hill, Richard Hinton, Johnny Hooker, Lewis Johnson, Mckenna Mahoney, David Mc Mahon, Purless Merrell, Horace Nelson, James Roberts, David Sanders, Robert Warren, Earl Williams, General Williams and Wilbert Williams.

Chapter 3

Military Years

Testing My Mettle

Warren Hope Dawson

Military Life - Below the Firing Line

I was commissioned as an officer in the United States Army in 1961. In August I reported to Fort Eustis, Virginia where I went through a six-week transportation officer's orientation course. In September, I entered active duty. In mid-October, I successfully completed the orientation course and was assigned to the 39th Transportation Battalion in Fort Benning, Georgia.

At Fort Benning, my unit was on alert for overseas movement. World attention was on the "Berlin Crisis." Aside from having to work a full military day (reveille, with morning calisthenics, and retreat), this alert situation meant I could not, or should not, buy the much desired first new automobile in my life. Sometime in mid-December of 1961, the alert was over, and I promptly bought myself a brand-new 1961 Chevrolet Corvair.

Yes, I finally had my new car, but even then, I knew I wanted to go to a law school. I also knew the debt related to the car payments could be at odds with my aspirations for a career in the law. So, to keep my law school option open, I was careful not to accumulate any debt that could not be fully paid by or before the expiration of my two-year military obligation. Also in this regard, I made the conscious decision to accumulate and save all my 60-day leave time. I preferred it be paid for at the end of my service. I followed my plan, and I received payment for the 59 days of leave I did not take.

While at Fort Benning, my unit was selected to participate in what was then known as the Third Army

Riot Control Troops. One of my assignments in this regard was to command and take a transportation unit to Fort McClellan, Alabama. Whenever you see the video footage from Birmingham, Alabama with the water hoses and attack dogs, I was one of the officers assigned to a task force drawn from several military bases and assembled at Fort McClellan, Alabama - an army post located near Birmingham.

We, as federal soldiers, had our own problems. While the horses and dogs were carrying on in the streets of Birmingham, we actually had one or more fights between blacks and whites on our military installation.

One of the internal fights happened at Task Force Headquarters and involved a black "buck" sergeant and a white "buck" sergeant. The two of them fought using their bayonets. We were lucky that no one died from "friendly fire."

Our Task Force was commanded by a Brigadier General who had come from the 101st Airborne Division at Fort Campbell, Kentucky. While we were on alert waiting to be called into Birmingham, we had several fights between black and white soldiers at Fort McClellan.

As for the other aspects of military life, few experiences made a greater impression on me than military training itself. I am not sure if they still perform this exercise, but there was one life-changing live-fire-drill designed to "test your mettle." A thirty caliber machine gun was mounted in a peak's position, and at night they would put you on the ground and have you crawl on your belly for approximately half the length of a football field. With the machine gun firing above your body, you could see the burning bullets flying by. In theory, you would have no problem, if you didn't panic, or stand up and if you kept your mind on what you were doing. As recently as 2014, I believe this training exercise was still being used. It was reported a young eighteen-year-old Florida trainee was killed during such an exercise.

A memorable and historic portion of my military years was my assignment in November of 1962 to participate in what became known as the Cuban Missile Crisis. My unit was dispatched from Fort Benning, Georgia down to what is now known as the Orlando International Airport. At the time, it was McCoy Air Force Base. Indeed, "MCO" are still the call letters for Orlando International.

At McCoy Air Force Base, my unit pitched tents right next to a runway. The U2 spy planes would run down the runway at night and return early in the morning, just around dawn. These planes were part of a mission to photograph what the Cubans were doing with missiles supplied by Russia. These were highly secretive flights and highly secretive airplanes. Our tents, mine included, were closer to the runway than most office buildings are to the street. In February of 1963, the Crisis was over, and it was time for my unit to return to Fort Benning, Georgia.

Before returning to Fort Benning, my final task was to transport, by truck, portions of a Field Army Hospital back to the Memphis Army Depot. I led a parade of trucks stretching approximately three miles long when traveling about 15 feet between vehicles. En route from Orlando, Florida to Memphis, Tennessee through the mountains. One of the stops along the way was Huntsville, Alabama. I remember Huntsville because the Redstone Arsenal is located there and is where, many years later my daughter,

Wendy lived.

On the way to Memphis, the men under my command and I consumed "C – Rations," the military's version of canned food. We were okay with canned food, but I speculated that if I could get my convoy to the civilian operated Memphis Army Depot before 5:00 p.m., I could get a hot meal for my men.

Unfortunately, we arrived at the depot too late for food. However, I spotted a restaurant just outside the depot and decided to feed my troops there. I had a military credit card and was prepared to buy all the food available to feed about seventy-five men.

When I entered the restaurant, in full military attire and with a host of military vehicles parked around the restaurant – I was met with these words: "I don't care who you are or what you want - you cannot come in here." Meaning, you may be a military officer and the commander of this unit, but you are black, and you cannot come in here.

Ultimately, I placed the need of my men for some hot food over this insult to my race and to my sacrifice for my country. I sent one of the white lieutenants under my command inside the restaurant to get all the hot food available. We consumed the food in our vehicles.

One night back in Fort Benning, Georgia, I was the staff duty officer. Being a young lieutenant and the staff duty officer for the night meant that from 6:30 in the evening until about 5:30 the next morning I was essentially in charge of the entire base. I was expected to stay up most of the night and be certain I knew who to call if something happened. Around 9:30 at night military installations were generally very quiet.

Then there was Phoenix City, Alabama. As a matter of fact, military guys visiting Phoenix City had a long history of problems, traceable all the way back to General George S. Patton. Patton had ordered Phoenix City off limits because military men were being taken advantage of there. Well, Phoenix City became my own Waterloo.

After I had finished all my assigned duties, I decided I really, really wanted to make a trip to Phoenix City. I simply told the sergeant I would be back. I took off my 45 pistol and left it there. I then drove my POV (Privately Owned Vehicle) over the back bridge into Phoenix City. I went to see someone I knew, and as I walked in the door, this person asked me to go to the corner store and get some Coca Cola.

I turned right around, got back in my car and drove down to the end of the street to a little mom and pop convenience store. This was long before the existence of 7-Eleven. I entered the store wearing all the stars, bars, and eagles I had, everything except my 45. As I walked in the store, I asked the man at the counter:

"Where are your Coca Colas?"

He said, "They're over there, Mac."

I said, "Sir, my name is not Mac. It's Dawson, see it right here on my fatigue?"

He didn't say a word. I found the sodas, came back in front to the counter, and put them down, and I asked:

"How much do I owe you?"

He said, "35 cents Mac."

I said, "Sir, I told you already my name is not Mac, okay. My name is Dawson."

My statement caused somebody, whom I had not noticed, to kick me from behind. You must remember, I was twenty one or twenty two years old and in good military shape. So, when I realized I had been kicked in the butt, I grabbed a nearby broom intending to slap whoever had kicked me. However, as I swirled around, the man behind the counter had picked up a forty five pistol (just like the one I left back at Fort Benning) and held it to my head – while saying: "Get your black ass out of this store, or I'll blow your head off and swear you were robbing the store."

The seventy five or eighty-year-old man, who had kicked me, was presumably the father of the man behind the counter. The son, who now had the gun to my head, walked me lock-step to the end of the counter and to the door. As I exited the door, the son kicked me so hard I went sliding to the ground of the unpaved parking lot. While the father had only lightly kicked me in the butt, the son must have been a high school field goal kicker.

The unpaved parking lot was covered with little sea shells, commonly used in small towns to cut down on dust on unpaved streets. Those shells cut my knees and hands.

Because I absolutely had no business being away from my military duty station (technically, I was absent without leave, commonly known as AWOL), I jumped in my car and returned to Fort Benning as fast as I could. My Phoenix City friend never saw me again, and I never saw Phoenix City again. I was just so happy to have escaped a serious situation that could have resulted in my death.

I am pleased to report I survived the military and

left active duty on August 29, 1963, the day after "The March on Washington." Indeed, I was on alert the day of The March, in the event federal troops were needed in Washington, DC.

The moment finally arrived for me to leave Fort Benning and head to Washington, DC to the Howard University School of Law. Also, the moment had arrived when I had to say goodbye to my shiny first automobile. I came face-to-face with the reality that both the car and I could not go to law school. So, I persuaded a sergeant in my unit to take over the payments. He drove me to the bus station.

As I boarded the Trailways bus, I gave the sergeant the keys to my car, along with the coupon payment book. I must confess, before the bus cleared the city limits of Columbus, Georgia, I shed some genuine tears over losing my first car. With those tears and the bus ride to Washington, DC, I transitioned from being an adult, a military officer, and a gentleman and returned to the status of being a student. A law student, yes, but still a student.

Chapter 4

Law School

Howard University Law School

Warren Hope Dawson at Howard University School of Law

In September 1963, just one week after living a soldier's life, I walked up to the window of the Registrar's office at Howard University to enroll in law school. I had roughly eleven hundred dollars in my pocket. I had my last Army paycheck of about three hundred and fifty dollars; A check for six hundred dollars, paid to me for fifty nine days of leave time I had not taken; and finally, a check for one hundred and fifty dollars for my travel expenses from Fort Benning, Georgia to Mulberry, Florida, my home of record. The military didn't consider where you were going, only where you came from. Mulberry, Florida was my home of record. I gave the Registrar seven hundred and six dollars of the eleven hundred dollars I had as my commitment to charting a new course for my life.

Next, I needed a job to accommodate my need to study and cover my living expenses. Fortunately, during that time frame, the Howard Law School allowed you to work – even during your first year. Before leaving Fort Benning, I had been in touch with the office of the senior United States Senator from Florida, Senator Spessard L. Holland. It just so happened, Senator Holland was from Bartow, Florida where I attended high school. Through his office, I was promptly hired to work for the Washington International Center.

My work hours were from 5:00 p.m. to 10:00 p.m. each night. My job duties consisted of going to the DC airports to meet and greet people coming to the United States under the Agency for International Development (AID) program. Upon their arrival, I proudly presented them with a taxi to a prearranged hotel, and their itinerary for the following morning. That job helped me do a lot of things I wanted to do, beyond what I had to do.

Life was good, and it got better in late November of 1963. The Ford Foundation then awarded a large grant to the Howard Law School. The seven hundred and six dollar enrollment fee I had paid in September, was fully refunded. The Ford grant funded my tuition, books and a small living stipend. The net effect of the grant was, my legal education was free. I was simply in the right place at the right time.

The grant, coupled with the pay from my night job, afforded me the opportunity to buy my second car. No, it was not new or shiny. It was an old 1954 Dodge that cost me all of three hundred dollars.

The car was another story. Oh, my God, the motor mounts were shot, and they basically hold the engine in the car. Therefore, the engine moved around, and that was not the only problem. One day, as I was heading south going over a big hill on Thirteenth St. in Washington, DC, I pumped the brake pedal, and the damn thing went all the way to the floor. I reached down to pull it back up, and the whole thing came up. I'm sitting there with the brake pedal in my hand, knowing I had to stop this car somehow. I managed to use a combination of emergency brakes and maneuvers to come to a stop, without hitting anyone.

Another problem was getting my blue baby started on cold mornings. I had an 8:00 a.m. class which made this an all-too-frequent and time-consuming task.

One morning I received a call and had to get going, quickly. Once it cranked up, I stopped on 14th street, which was between where I lived and the law school. It was 7:00 a.m., and I wanted a sausage sandwich. Because that was all the breakfast, I would have, with no McDonald's, and no sausage and cheese biscuits, it was routine to stop at an old greasy spoon and get myself a sandwich.

On this particular morning, I was afraid to turn off the engine because it might not crank up again. But, I was going to get that sandwich. Meanwhile, unlike today, Howard Law School had no parking. There was simply nowhere to park. It was not uncommon to acquire two parking tickets per day.

To my horror, when I came out and walked around to get back in the car, a motorcycle cop was standing there with my keys in his hand. With fifty nine prior parking tickets with my name on them, I knew I was done.

To my amazement, he said he would not give me a ticket and would let me go if I didn't have any other tickets. God forgive me for I said, "No, I absolutely don't have any other tickets." So he said, "Oh alright, let me go down to this call box." The technology of 1963 was to go to a call box and call the office where someone would manually check local records. There were no computers, and at 7:00 a.m., the office had not yet opened.

If this had happened in a later era, when he asked me if I had any tickets, I would have walked down to this officer trying to surrender. Well, it wasn't necessary. He came back and brought me the ticket with a "leaving the keys in the car" violation, and told me I could go.

Then came a day, when I visited a friend who lived in a posted parking area. It clearly warned parking was only permitted until 7:00 a.m. By morning, deliveries were being made, and you needed to be long gone. Somehow, I managed not to get out of there by 7:00.

When I came out, the car was gone. Since I had enough parking tickets and other parking fees that would equal four times the value of the car, I quickly recognized it didn't make any sense to even think about trying to get the car back.

As for the law student experience, Howard students met some rather extraordinary people. In October of 1963, my classmates and I were invited to Bobby Kennedy's personal office, the Attorney General of United States and President John F. Kennedy's brother. We spent about ninety minutes talking about the President, who in less than a month later was assassinated. Unfortunately, while we were in the Attorney General's office, one aggressive classmate, Charles Jones, was making such outrageous and disrespectful statements Bobby Kennedy snapped and said to him, "You don't know my brother that well to be talking about him like that." This was a hard lesson in decorum for Charles Jones. Learning took place for us in and out of the classroom.

Sometimes, as was the case during my undergraduate years, our winter and summer vacation breaks were themselves rather exciting. My childhood friend, Bobby Gene White, was the source of considerable adventure. Bobby was one of my earliest and influential contemporaries, and I was extremely impressed with how he dressed. So much so, I was willing to follow him into dangerous situations. Unfortunately, a great deal of what he had, he stole.

There were a couple of men's stores in Lakeland, Florida, one called Streamline and another store that I can't recall its name. We would walk in and try on a pair of pants. If they fit, we put our pants back on over the new pants and walk out of the store. By the Grace of God, we did this many times and without getting caught.

After high school, Bobby, like most others, went to work in the phosphate mines. His whole world was right there in Mulberry and Bartow. So, when I came home from law school and spent time with my friend, I was talking about things he found hard to believe.

To prove the point that things had changed, I stopped him from going around to the back of the restaurant we were approaching by saying, "I don't know if you know it or not, but we can go in the front of the restaurant now!" So, we entered the front door and sat down.

Five minutes later, the Mulberry police showed up in full force. It was a two-step process to make an arrest in little Mulberry back then. First, the police had to call for a county deputy sheriff. When the sheriff arrived, I worked psychological magic on him with information which was about ninety percent true. I said, "Hey, I'm so glad to see you. I am aware these Mulberry policemen don't know about this new law, but as the deputy sheriff, I know you know."

I continued, "I came home from Washington, DC, where I attend law school. I know you must know U.S. Senator Spessard L. Holland, who grew up right here in Bartow. My mother used to work for him (not true). Well, he was directly responsible for my being hired in DC and is the reason I am in law school."

The deputy sheriff was eating everything I was telling him. I said, "When I get back, I will tell Senator Holland how you resolved this situation. In, fact what is your name?" Without hesitation, the deputy sheriff gave me his full name. With that, I succeeding in getting him to release us - with the expectation that I would favorably mention his name to Senator Holland.

During the Christmas vacation in 1964, I traveled by train from Washington, DC to Florence, South Carolina to visit my grandmother in Darlington. Florence was a major train stop for service and maintenance. On my return to Washington, my aunt, Ruth Warren, drove me from Darlington back to Florence. While it was only ten miles and the train didn't leave until 11:30 p.m., my aunt, because of her age and eyesight, did not drive after dark. So, she dropped me off at about 6:00 p.m. and I waited for nearly five hours for the train to arrive.

Around 8:30 p.m., I was truly hungry and noticed a restaurant directly across the street from the train station. As there were no restaurants in the train station, I headed over to get something to eat. As I opened the door of the restaurant, a man was leaving. As I approached the counter, the waiter yelled, "Can I help you?" I interpreted his action as an effort to stop me before I reached the stools in front of the counter. Since I knew well that the 1964 Civil Rights Act had recently passed, I ignored the waiter and continued to the counter and seated myself on one of the stools. Once seated, I said, "I want a hamburger."

About ten white men were sitting at the counter and watched this scene unfold. Before I could finish ordering the hamburger, I heard gunshots: "Bang, bang, bang." With my back turned, someone was firing a gun directly behind me. At that point, I could have already have been a dead man. Fortunately however, I was only a year or so removed from active military service, and from the sound of the gunshots I immediately recognized the person was firing blanks.

After I turned around, I also recognized that the man who had fired the shots was the same man who was leaving the restaurant as I entered. Apparently, he had gone directly to his car and retrieved a revolver.

When I rose from the counter and faced him, he then abandoned the gun and approached me with the intent of taking me on physically. We were about to go at it when four or five white men jumped up and stood between us. More than one of them politely suggested to me that I should leave before I get hurt.

Having already thoroughly pissed off one white man merely by my presence, I decided it was in my best interest (both short run and long term) to accept their advice. So, I left.

The driveway in front of the train station was a semi-circle. As I approached the station, I realized the aggressor was now in his car and determined to run over me. I reached into my winter coat as if to pull out a gun. He put on brakes. When he did, I ran. I ran through the station and across the tracks to hide. I waited there, in the cold, for the train to arrive. When my train finally pulled into the station, the doors opened, on the opposite side. I was on the track side where the doors remained closed. I banged on the door until someone opened it and let me in.

It was Christmas time and cold, which usually meant I was about to experience some of the best sleep ever.

There is nothing better than the steam heat from a train on a winter night. But on that night, as I sank into the safety of my seat and realized what I had just been through, my eyes were like saucers. I couldn't sleep at all. Please know, that to this day, I never sit in a restaurant with my back to the door.

> ♪ **"His eye is on the sparrow
> and I know he is watching me"** ♪

The Florence, South Carolina experience gave me a greater appreciation for two of my Howard Law School classmates: Ezell Blair, Jr. and Bobby Hill. Before law school, Hill had been a national president of the NAACP Youth Movement. Blair had been one of the young men at North Carolina A&T University, in Greensboro, North Carolina, who started the lunch counter sit-in demonstrations in 1960. Blair and Hill were the John Lewis' of their states.

Fellow students were not the only ones who went on to make history. Professor Howard Jenkins, one of our black law professors who taught part-time, was a member of the National Labor Relations Board (NLRB). The first black member of that five-member board.

Member Jenkins was directly connected to my being hired by the NLRB. I was hired in Washington, DC through Member Jenkins' office and sent to work for the NLRB in Tampa. At the time (1966), it would have been political suicide for the head of the Tampa regional office of NLRB to hire me - a black law graduate. The national pressure on the local branch would have been intense. On June 13, 1966, I arrived and went to work for the NLRB on the seventh floor of the Timberlake Federal Building, located at 500 Zack Street, Tampa Florida. I was the only black person working in the building.

Charles Hamilton Houston served as Vice-Dean and then Dean of the Howard University School of Law from 1929-35. In that capacity, he had direct influence on nearly one-quarter of all the black lawyers in the United States, including former student Thurgood Marshall. Houston had the notion that a lawyer should also be a social engineer.

It was at the Howard Law School where most of the major civil rights cases were pre-argued prior to being argued before the U.S. Supreme Court. Indeed, the famous case of <u>Brown vs. The Board of Education</u>, 347 U.S. 483 (1954) was not only pre-argued but was largely prepared by lawyers who had some affiliation with the Howard Law School. They included: Thurgood Marshall, James M. Nabrit, Jr., George E.C. Hayes, Oliver Hill, Spottswood Robinson, III and others.

This process also created interest in public service and an environment where Frank Reeves, the first black Commissioner of the District of Columbia government, was appointed. If you look closely at the Washington, DC flag, you will notice it has three stars. It has a white background with three red stars, and I suggest ninety seven percent of the people who live in the District have no idea what those three stars stand for. I know.

The three stars are for the Commissioners who served the District of Columbia during the early years. They served when the government of the District of Columbia laws allowed for an elected person, and an appointed person with the three commissioners, one of them was a general who headed the U.S. Army engineering core.

When Commissioner Reeves was appointed by President John Kennedy, it was the first time one of those stars stood for a black man. Reeves was a professor at the Howard University Law School. Unfortunately, he had done some things before he took office and did not serve out of his term. Reeves was replaced by Walter Washington, who later became the first elected DC mayor.

The United States finally gave in to DC on December 24, 1973, with the District of Columbia Home Rule Act. That "home rule" act allowed DC to elect certain officials, including a mayor and members of the Council. Soon thereafter, people like Marion Barry and others were elected. DC has a non-voting delegate in the U.S. House, like the U.S. Virgin Islands and other U.S. territories. DC has no presence in the U.S. Senate.

With studies completed, law school graduation day finally arrived. Congressman Adam Clayton Powell, Jr. was the 1966 Howard University commencement speaker. On most days, this charismatic New York congressman was a theatrical Baptist church preacher. However, on this day, there was extra drama, because he had come to Howard on a mission: to remind the university officials of how powerful he was.

Consider that there were only two non-military universities in the nation primarily funded by the federal government, i.e. Howard University and Gallaudet University. Howard was created and funded to educate the mulatto offspring of unions between white men and black women. Gallaudet was created and funded to educate the deaf. Both schools are in Washington, DC. The federal funding that came to these universities originated in the Education and Labor Committee of the U.S. House of Representatives. That committee was then chaired by Congressman Powell.

To further understand the scenario: for years Howard University, one of the major beneficiaries of his power, had not invited him to speak at commencement. To say he was pissed, without apology, would be a major understatement.

After years of perceived insults, Powell came that early morning in 1966 to an outdoor Howard commencement ceremony truly pissed off at Howard. As a preacher, his presentation was a commencement sermon as well as a commencement speech. The subject of his sermon was "Is There Any Good Thing Coming Out of Howard?" Thus, he was paralleling the story of Sodom and Gomorrah to lambaste the university administration for taking so long to invite him to speak. The general wickedness of their ways, his speech seemed to imply, surely deserved a more severe punishment than the tongue lashing they received.

For visual impact, Powell's complexion and hair made him appear to be white. Given he looked white, Powell went to extremes to make sure you knew he was black. The visual of the day put an exclamation mark on the scene for the wind was blasting – making it necessary for Powell to constantly toss the hair back off his face as he was speaking. It was a sight to behold. I marvel to this day that Adam Clayton Powell Jr. spoke at my law school graduation commencement. What a poignant moment.

There indeed was another connection between Adam Clayton Powell and Howard. Mr. Herbert O. Reid, one of my law professors, was Powell's main counsel in the famous case known as Powell vs. McCormack. That case, before the U.S. Supreme Court, involved Powell's successful effort, in 1967, to overturn the action of his House colleagues that kicked him out of Congress. Prominent among Powell's colleagues who pushed and voted for his ouster was Sam Gibbons, the Congressman from Tampa, Florida.

Thirty-five years later, as President of the National Bar Association, I recognized Herbert O. Reid with the highest award of the National Bar Association: The C. Francis Stradford Award.

Major events in my life occurred in the good year of 1966. I finished law school in June and I married my wife-for-life in August. Joan Delores Brown, originally of New Bern, North Carolina, was living in Washington, DC and teaching in the school system of Arlington County, Virginia. We were introduced to each other by Harris Bostic, one of my law school classmates. We dated during my senior year at Howard. Joan became a good wife and a real partner who remained there for me through the ups and downs that visit every marriage. I am, and will be, eternally grateful to her for having been an essential part of my life.

As indicated, I came out of the Howard Law School in 1966 and went near home to Tampa, Florida, a town in which no black person had been elected to anything: My entire Howard experience, the people I met and the examples put before me, motivated me to change Tampa's history.

Several of my Howard schoolmates from Georgia, South Carolina, and other places were going back home and getting elected to public office. Bobby Hill from Savannah, Georgia, Benjamin Brown from Atlanta, Georgia, and others. Since they were going back to their hometowns and native states getting elected to office, I saw a need in Tampa, and I became laser focused on making it possible for blacks to get elected in Tampa.

Indeed that election thing became a major piece of my life. Despite my support, involvement, and participation in getting representation for black people, personally, it proved to be the most elusive thing in my whole career. Nevertheless, I did succeed in having laws and policies changed so that representation for black people could happen. I never succeeded in getting elected, and as I said; that's rather a separate story.

When I graduated from law school in 1966, the records indicated that The Florida Bar was apparently committed to the proposition that only two blacks would be allowed to pass the Bar Exam - no matter how many blacks took it.

> ♪ *"We have come this far by faith leaning on the Lord"* ♪

The Bar Exam was given twice a year. Studying for the exam was a little bit different and more onerous than most exams. People studied for the exam, essentially for a three to five-week period, not knowing whether it's night or day. They were consumed with studying. They sat through refresher courses by day and studied with a partner or alone by night.

It was especially difficult to spend all that time studying for something when you knew or felt somebody had a thumb on the scale. It was a major mental chore to concentrate, thinking you may not pass the exam because you're black, no matter your score. If you doubt the system, and you may have good reason to do so, how do you continue to prepare and study so maybe you can pass? The answer is: you must have the strength of body and mind, the kind I experienced when I completed the Army drill of crawling under live machine gun night fire. I was simply determined to become a lawyer – no matter what. My thought was: "If they're only going to allow two black people to pass, then I intend to be one of the two."

I didn't pass the first time and received these unforgettable words:

> WESTERN UNION:
> MAY 22 1967
> WARREN HOPE DAWSON
> 4219 LAUREL ST. TAMPA FL
>
> REGRET YOU WERE UNSUCCESSFUL ON MARCH BAR EXAMINATION. LETTER OF CONFIRMATION FOLLOWS
>
> FLORIDA BOARD OF BAR EXAMINERS.

I passed the second time and received these extraordinary words:

> WESTERN UNION:
> OCT 30 1967
> WARREN HOPE DAWSON
> 4219 LAUREL ST. TAMPA FL
>
> YOU PASSED BAR EXAMINATION.
>
> CONGRATULATIONS.
>
> INDUCTION CEREMONIES IN MIAMI, LAKELAND, VERO BEACH, AND TALLAHASSE, NOVEMBER 10. LETTER FOLLOWS
>
> FLORIDA BOARD OF BAR EXAMINERS.

♪ *"Victory, victory shall be mine*
If hold my peace
and let the Lord fight my battles-
victory, victory shall be mine" ♪

The Journey of an African Legal Eagle 89

Howard University School of Law - Class of 1966 including Warren Hope Dawson

Warren Hope Dawson & The Honorable Thurgood Marshall

♪ *"Lord I'm running trying to make 100 'cause 99 1/2 won't do"* ♪

Howard University Law Alumni Association

In the late 1980s, through to 1990, I had the high honor of serving as National President Howard University Law Alumni Association. As you can imagine, this historically significant law school contributed more than its share of graduates who distinguished themselves in the law as lawyers and judges. To mention a few: Thurgood Marshall, Justice, Supreme Court of the United States; Spottswood W. Robinson III, Judge, U.S. Court of Appeals for the District of Columbia Circuit; Damon J. Keith, Judge, U. S. Court of Appeals for the Sixth Circuit; Joseph Hatchett, Judge of the U.S. Court of Appeals for the Eleventh Circuit; Thomas James (T.J.) Cunningham, Cunningham & Cunningham Law Firm; Vernon Jordon, Akin Gump Law Firm; Douglass Wilder, Governor of Virginia; Leander J. Shaw Jr., Supreme Court of Florida; Adolpho A. Birch Jr., Supreme Court of Tennessee; Ralph D. Cook, Supreme Court of Alabama; Wayman Smith III, Vice President Anheuser-Busch; Gabrielle Kirk McDonald, Judge, International Criminal Tribunal for the former Yugoslavia; J. Clay Smith Jr., Chair, Equal Employment Opportunity Commission; Togo D. West, Jr., Secretary, U.S. Army and Sharon Pratt Kelly, Mayor Washington D C.

During the several years of my presidency, it was my pleasure to work with the Dean, the administration, the faculty and the student body to sustain and improve upon the contributions this unique law school has made to the rule of law and the legal profession, since its beginning in 1869.

My Competitive Nature

By the time the world considered me to be an adult, I had an unshakable competitive spirit traceable back to as early as my junior high school days, if not before.

Unfortunately, I was never athletically inclined. Sure, I played on the playground just like any other kid. However, regarding being good enough to play on a team, of any kind, I was never any good. Even when it came to intramural play, where kids picked sides to form teams, I was the kid who was never picked – and they had a good reason. No one wanted me on their team. I was even more left out when it came to teams with coaches. The closest I ever came was they would use me as a show piece in junior high school basketball because of my height, but of course, number fifteen (my number) never found its way onto the court.

As mentioned when recalling my interaction with Mr. Simmons and his displeasure with my calling the softball game, I also offer that event as an example of my competitive nature.

My cultivated knack for finding a way to get-into-the-game continued into my high school years. I tried out for football but had a big problem getting into shape. In those days, black schools did not have weights for conditioning, so we used calisthenics. Unfortunately, by the time we finished exercising, I was done.

The combination of the 4:00 p.m. Florida summer heat;

the ground with little grass; the firecracker hot sand; and the small patches of grass, generously infected with sand spurs, created a challenge I could not handle. Suffice to say; I didn't get very far playing high school football. However, as in junior high school, I did find a way to get-into-the-game. I became a sports writer covering my school's football games for a newspaper.

I was a paper boy delivering newspapers for the Florida Sentinel, the Tampa Bulletin, and the Pittsburgh Courier. I connected with the Florida Sentinel to write a sports article for the newspaper. That earned a spot for me on the bus with the basketball team. Even though I wasn't a player, I still found a way to get-into-the-game, because I was the reporter.

In eleventh grade, I did what few other people can claim. I applied for, took, and passed the "game official's test" for basketball. In the twelfth-grade, I became a certified game official in basketball. I was not a player but once again I found a way to get-into-the-game.

One night at Union Academy High School in Bartow, my high school, was playing Pinellas High School, the black high school from Clearwater. I was there as a student with my game official's card in my pocket. The game was supposed to start at 7:00 p.m., but an hour later the game had not started.

Unknown to us sitting in the stands, one of the game officials assigned to this game had been involved in an automobile accident. To solve the problem, the Union Academy coach, Forrest McKennie, approached the coach from Pinellas High and made three suggestions. (1) That the game be canceled; (2) that the game proceed with the one game official; or (3) that the game proceed using the assigned official and a student who was a certified game official. That would be me!

When I learned that the game could be canceled, due to the absence of the second official, I produced my certification to both coaches, and it was accepted. That placed me, as a student, in the most unlikely and unique status of having to help referee a basketball game that involved the high school in which I was a student.

As the game proceeded, I quickly recognized that when I was in doubt, I would make the call against my own school trying to go overboard to show my fairness. An approach or practice that I later despised in some black judges. In any event, I once again had found a way to get-into-the-game.

True to my nature, the competitive thing continued into college. I found a way to get into the world famous marching band at Florida A&M University. Now, I didn't play an instrument and had never marched in a band. However, after I surveyed and closely studied the cymbal players I said to myself, "I think I can do that." I prepared myself to take on the cymbals, but before that plan played out, the school indicated that the band needed a public-address announcer. Please know that I said to all who would listen, "I KNOW I CAN DO THAT!"

I auditioned and became the "Voice of the Marching 100." The long-termed founder and director of the band, Dr. William Patrick Foster, said to me and others, he had never had an announcer who was better than Dawson. Once again, I had found a way to get-into-the-game.

My competitive nature and my finding a way to get involved continued after college and on into life. In fact, my competitive spirit led me to believe I could effectively do the work of both the President of the United States and the work of a back-of-the-truck garbage man. My thought was, due to the physical and strenuous nature of the job, I probably would need about three weeks to get in shape to be able to jump up on a truck, jump down, pick up a can, and throw it on to the truck and then jump back up on the truck.

On the other hand, when I compared the qualifications of U.S. Presidents George W. Bush, Ronald Reagan, and Donald Trump, I was convinced I would need no advanced time at all to prepare. I don't have that exact feeling as it relates to President Barack Obama and his superior intellect.

Chapter 5

Launching A Career

In Tampa Florida

"The ability to read and write effectively and to think logically is critical irrespective of one's career choice."

A number of factors came together to support my initial career efforts. When I arrived in Tampa, the primary welcome mat came from C. Blythe Andrews Sr., publisher and owner of the Florida Sentinel Newspaper. In the early days he wrote a column himself called "So They Tell Me." By way of background my mother, Naomi Warren Dawson, and I distributed the paper in Polk County. Thus taking it beyond Tampa made true the Sentinel's claim of being a "Floridian" paper.

Appreciating the past and understanding my potential, In 1968, Andrews Sr. wrote the following words in his column:

> *Atty. Warren Dawson*
> *It was a pleasure and honor to visit the well appointed and plush office of Atty. Warren Dawson, located in the complex recently built at 3518 29th Street, Tampa, by Dr. J. O. Brookins, one of your outstanding medical leaders.*
>
> *Atty Dawson is the son of Mrs. Naomi Dawson White, pioneer leader of Polk County and one of the people who helped to build the Florida Sentinel Bulletin.*
>
> *Atty. Dawson is a graduate of Florida A. & M. University and the Law College of Howard University. He's a gifted public speaker and probably would enjoy appearing on your program.*

Appointed Assistant City Attorney

It was early in 1968, with the blessings of City Attorney, William Reece Smith, Jr., Mayor Dick Greco appointed me Assistant City Attorney. At the time, only the Chief Assistant City Attorney worked out of City Hall. The City Attorney and the other assistants worked out of their private offices. My office was located at 3556 N. 29th Street, and I served the City from that office.

"Project Pride," a housing rehabilitation activity partially funded by the Federal Government, was one of my first assignments. The Federal Government would award loans and grants to people in certain designated neighborhoods to rehabilitate their property. The legal work in this "Project" focused on preparing mortgages for the loans given to people for the rehabilitation.

Eventually, there came a need to develop a minimum housing code not just for the areas covered by "Project Pride" (which was largely Ybor City) but also for the entire city. I was given the task. The earliest minimum housing code for the City of Tampa was developed by me; so, I might be referred to as the father of the minimum housing code for the City of Tampa.

A part of my duties, as Assistant City Attorney, was to enforce the minimum housing code. The Tampa Stetson Law Center now sits where the Police Station was, which housed the Municipal City Court of Tampa. It was in that court that I was a prosecutor. I prosecuted minimum housing code violations for about four to five years before I resigned to run for The Florida Legislature.

Looking back, I recall a few fascinating moments as Assistant City Attorney; one had to do with Muhammad Ali. It was about 1970, and around the time Muhammad Ali was stripped of his title for refusing to serve in the United States Military. He was not allowed to fight anywhere. There were several attempts around the country to get a venue for Ali to fight an exhibition fight. All the public venues turned him down, and Tampa was no exception.

Ali was trying to get the Old Curtis Hixon Hall, and on the day his request was heard by the City Council, I went down and put my two cents worth in. I argued Ali should be allowed to fight an exhibition in Tampa at Curtis Hixon. Of course, his request was denied.

Shortly thereafter, I gave an interview in which I said I thought there was an element of racism involved in the refusal. This having been said, and probably printed in the paper, I promptly received a call from the City Attorney who, reminded me the City was my client and I had just called them racist. Fortunately, the City Attorney was very liberal and one who was not inclined to be punitive towards me.

The City of Orlando did allow an Ali exhibition fight and became the stage for my personal Muhammad Ali story. My friend, Tommy Martin, and I went to the fight. The security for Ali and the fight itself was handled by Muslims of which about ten of them were from Tampa and several knew me. The leader came up to me and asked if I was going to the post-fight dinner with the champ. I knew nothing about this but said sure.

When I arrived, the guys who had invited me were there and, someone instructed me to "sit right here." I did as I was instructed. However, there was a very pretty woman sitting in the adjacent seat. A short time later Ali, who had showered and changed, walked up to me and asked, "Why are you sitting in my seat?" The woman was his girlfriend at the time who later became his wife.

Also during my tenure as City Attorney, there had not been any black person elected to any office in Hillsborough County since the late 1880s. That, to me, was a very frustrating problem I felt some responsibility to correct. The City Clerk was elected during that time-frame, (now

1967 Lawyer Swearing-In Ceremony for the Second District Court of Appeal of Florida.

The Journey of an African Legal Eagle 101

If there had to be "only one" black attorney admitted to the Bar that day, indeed it would be me, Warren Hope Dawson.

this office is filled by appointment). Just for comparison and reference, and not to minimize the office, you might say this was the lowest official office in the city.

When it came time to elect, or reelect, the City Clerk, I publicly backed Bobby Thompson, a native of Tampa, a college basketball player and one of the first black men hired to sell insurance locally for a large insurance company comparable to AETNA and New York Life.

I gave Bobby the money to qualify, and his report revealed the only money he had essentially backing him came from my donation. Suffice to say, once again the City Attorney contacted me (by letter this time) again informing me the City was my client; therefore, in essence, all of its officials were my clients as well.

My response was, while Mr. Starks as the City Clerk was my client, he was not my client in his endeavor to remain the City Clerk. I further declared, I personally had the right to vote for and to support anyone I chose. My argument prevailed.

I am reasonably certain, in 1967, I was the first black Assistant City Attorney in the entire South. Nine years later in 1976, George F. Knox became the City Attorney in Miami.

Private Practice

The law offices of Warren Hope Dawson opened on January 1, 1968, which was the genesis of my fifty plus years in the private practice of law in my beloved adopted city, Tampa, Florida.

Being in private practice had its challenges and its rewards. What follows are stories of some incredible heart-stopping and extremely frightening moments I cannot forget:

The Approach – After a mentally grueling day, I stopped by a local lounge for a drink and to wind down. This day was no different than any other day until a friend of mine, who just happened to be there, tapped me on the back.

He motioned for me to follow him, in a way that was alarming. I did. Then he revealed, indeed, he had moved me out of harm's way.

He told me a man had been standing directly behind me with a deliberate intent to do me harm. My friend told me the man said I had handled a case against one of his close relatives. The man wanted revenge.

Cadillac Eldorado Convertible - I was riding with the top down and enjoying the breeze when I looked to my left and down the barrel of a gun.

A car had pulled up parallel to me and a man was pointing a gun right at my head. I wasted no time trying to determine who this was or the nature of his anger. I put the petal to the metal which felt like a scene from a bad movie.

The car sped up with the intent to remain parallel to me. I slammed on the brakes. He did too. While he was maneuvering to get back to me, I took a hard right and went down another street and managed to get away from this mad man.

He was white. However, I have no idea if he was angry about my car, with this black man driving it, or if he knew me and had a meaningful grudge against me. This was about the time when I was heavily and publicly involved in all sorts of civil rights cases and activities. It was not uncommon to hear about someone being shot or bombed. This was a real threat to my life.

Bad Blacks - Some people show their admiration for others by clipping news articles about their accomplishments and sending the articles to them. By doing so, they are letting them know they are celebrating their success.

There is another group of people out there who use this technique in quite a different manner. I became the face of the black community and the subject of community hate mail. Frequently, when a black person who did something terrible was written about in the news, I received a copy of the article.

The article arrived at my office, from an anonymous source, with a note informing me this was the reason I, and all my people, should go back to Africa. My actions and my address were public. I was a convenient and easy target.

Really Lady? - A potential client arrived in my office determined to file a discrimination suit against the

Mulberry police. She angrily told me how her star high school quarterback son was discovered in a compromised situation with a white girl.

The police confronted her seventeen-year-old son, who was in the back woods, in the dark, and with a white girl. The boy's mother wanted to file a suit because the policeman called her son a nigger. All I could think of was "really lady?" Given the times, her son was REALLY lucky to be alive.

In my private practice I was largely pleased to work with the following lawyers and law clerks: Prince McIntosh, Kenneth Glover, Robert Morrison, Patricia Dawson, Eric Myers, Debra Glover, Alfred Wells, Eurich Griffin, Christopher Clark, Treveno Gaylord, Hewitt Smith, Iyada Jackson, Monica McCoy, Bridget Scott, Shameka Askew, and Isaac Ruiz-Cruz.

This Journey would have been mission impossible but for the able assistance of my office assistants over the years that have included: Betty Davis, Pat Towns, Henrie Mae Phillips Dorothy Garrick, Tiffany Judge and Dorothy Buster.

HOBA or TOBA

History is shaped by those who tell it. Sometimes storytellers get it right and sometimes they do not. At first, it may be known to be incorrect, and later the truth lay buried beneath generations of time. Such is the case of the birth of Tampa Organization of Black Affairs (TOBA). Today it is reported to have been founded by some people who were physically situated within five feet, or less, of my office and me. I suggest TOBA's history, as reported, is inaccurate.

Prior to the celebrated origin of TOBA, there was Hillsborough County Organization of Black Affairs (HOBA). Even though it may never be uncovered, I'm betting there is media coverage contemporaneous with its formation. On the other hand, I contend there is no media coverage validating the claimed date of TOBA's formation.

With the recognized founders of TOBA working out of my law office and the law office next door, it is unreasonable to believe I was not involved. Excuse me! The idea I was not involved is really a form of history re-write and self-promotion to exclude me from a deserved place in Tampa's history.

Hillsborough County Organization of Black Affairs is an activity I thought about as I sat on the seventh floor of the Timberlake Federal Building located at 500 Zack Street in downtown Tampa, Florida, where I first reported on the 13th day of June of 1966.

I was reading the newspaper and recognized we had what was known as multi-member districts in the Florida legislature. Multi-member districts in the legislature meant a particular area would have a set of representatives. For example, Hillsborough at that time was allocated eight representatives - all running at large.

The article revealed they were strategizing about adding three more counties, Pasco, Citrus, and Hernando to the district. The plan was to add those counties and three more seats so there would be eleven district representatives from this area. If adopted, the change would include all of Hernando, all of Citrus, all of Pasco and all of Hillsborough Counties and have a total of eleven representatives.

The plan was to appropriate the three new seats to three added counties. Although the population and votes in Hillsborough County were sufficient to elect candidates from Hillsborough to the three new seats, the plan was to urge the Hillsborough voters to vote for candidates from the three added counties – so that those counties could have representation – despite their small population.

Well, my being fresh out of law school, I was familiar with the United States Supreme Court case of Baker vs. Carr, 369 U.S. 186 (1962). The case concerned "one man one vote"; meaning the representation should be where the people are, not where the pine trees are, not where the cattle are, not where the land is, not where the governmental unit like a county or city, or town is but where the people are.

Therefore, if the people, in this instance, were in Hillsborough County, which they were and far outnumbered those three counties, then the representation ought to be essentially where the people are.

The argument from the Florida perspective was each county needed its own statement on the floor of the House to speak for a county or its town or group of towns. That was contrary to "one man - one vote" which said no counties may need representations. The real representation should be for the people. Therefore, wherever the people are is where the representation should be.

The black population in Tampa was almost equal to the total population black and white in those three counties. Unlike today, those counties were very under populated. Back then there were more black people in certain areas of Hillsborough County than there were people total in those three counties combined.

I said, "I'm not from here, and I'm just the new person in town. But that sounds wrong to me." I called a meeting, rallying some black people interested in doing or saying something about the problem. I scheduled the room, called the meeting and the word spread. People came.

I called the activity the Hillsborough County Organization of Black Affairs (HOBA) designed to confront the media and the existing legislative delegation about this idea floated by the media, "We in Hillsborough County should not be so greedy as to gobble up these three new seats simply because we had the votes to do it" was the theme of the media coverage.

As expected, the media showed up and prevailed upon the voting delegation to do exactly what they asked them to do. As a result, John R. Culbreath and Thomas A. Stevens were elected to represent the three counties added to this House District.

The face of the "media" was primarily that of the publisher and chairman of the editorial board of the Tampa Tribune Newspaper, James Clendenen. He was adamantly opposed to anything he called "ward politics" or anything that suggested single-member districts. The Tribune owned another daily called the Tampa Times, the afternoon paper.

Although I was still working for the NLRB, I did call a meeting. We formalized our complaints and developed a strategy as HOBA. Then we met with the legislative delegation.

After we met with the legislative delegation and voiced our opposition to this multi-member district addition of new representatives to cover the three additional counties, the media picked it up. Somehow, the media coverage caught the attention of the NLRB, my employer, headquarters in Washington, DC.

This drew attention because a federal law existed for many years called the Hatch Act. It may have come from Orrin Hatch, a senator from Utah. The Hatch Act says simply; a government employee should not engage in partisan politics.

Frankly, this was never about politics. I think this is where my mouth and my party were perceivably inseparable. My pitch was, blacks saw no justice in giving away seats to people simply because they live in Pasco, Citrus and Hernando counties when black folks live right here in Hillsborough County where the votes are. There was no justice where blacks didn't have any legislative representation at all, and they were proposing to give it to land and cows.

Next thing I knew, I received word from Washington, "I think you might be engaging in partisan politics and that would be a violation of Hatch Act." I stepped back and said let me get somebody else to be the spokesman. I was not elected to an official position, but I was the lead spokesperson.

My original and personal idea was to challenge this publicly and assemble the fathers of several cities and local black leaders. I did so as a very young man of twenty eight years old. These were men who were very prominent in this town: like Perry Harvey Sr. and C. Blythe Andrews Sr. I was on average, ten years younger than their sons.

After the Hatch Act issue was raised, it was Perry Harvey Sr. who I asked to take over the responsibility of being the visible spokesperson for HOBA. In his own style, Mr. Harvey Sr., who had two well-educated sons, went out of his way to challenge "college-educated men."

The night we had a little meeting, and Mr. Harvey was going be asked to be the spokesperson, the discussion went something like this. He referred to me as, "This little faggot right here." Remember, I wasn't even his son's age. I was 10 years younger than his son. I assumed, given the times, this was Harvey's acknowledgment I was young and yet calling the shots. In some ways, a form of saying this skinny, young, educated boy had arrived since I was going toe to toe with him.

These activities laid the groundwork for the ritual of the upcoming census where we were to make reapportionments. A process the legislature in every state and the Congress of United States engages in every ten years. Congress takes the results of the last census to reconfigure the electoral districts. Therefore, this is all about reapportionment.

The reapportionment in the district of Florida said we needed to add three more seats to these areas which included Hillsborough, Pasco Citrus, and Hernando. We didn't fail. They eventually did reapportion it and added more seats for blacks. My protest, initiative and leadership set the stage for later change. The system didn't change until long after I left the NLRB. In fact, it was under the single-member district system I first ran for the legislature.

♪ *"Trouble in my way,*
I had to cry sometime
- but Jesus will fix it after while" ♪

National Bar Association

I had been an active member of the National Bar Association (NBA) for several years before I ran for an office. I served as vice president for a few years then ran for president-elect. In hindsight, I probably should have run for president-elect several years earlier than I did.

In 1978, I was elected vice president, and my assigned responsibility was to increase membership from 10,000 members. I set my sights on recruiting and making active every black lawyer in the United States. During my two-year tenure as vice president, I increased the membership by 2000 new members, which influenced my decision to run for president.

In 1980, I had planned for more than a year to run for president-elect at the annual meeting of the Bar Association's National Convention held at the Fairmount Hotel in Dallas, Texas. Until this time, there had never been a woman president of this organization of lawyers, judges, law professors and law students. My opponent was a woman lawyer from Chicago and my response to her candidacy was: while I supported the idea of a woman president, but "not this year." I lost.

In those days, the Association's election results were not reported out until just before the closing banquet. There literally was about one hour before you found out if you had won or lost. After receiving the news of my defeat, I went to my suite and ordered dinner for my family and closest friends because I wasn't going to attend that banquet.

We had consumed only a portion of our meal when O.T. Wells, a past president from the State of New York, told me the Closing Banquet had started and that I should come down. He reasoned that it would be an "act of concession" and it would demonstrate strength and commitment to take the loss. When I entered the banquet, I received a standing ovation.

As I set on the dais in my capacity as Vice President, many lawyers came up to me and said just run again the next year at our Convention in Detroit. However, before the night was over, someone came up to me and informed me that Dennis Archer, a very prominent lawyer from Detroit, would also be a candidate for NBA President. Renee Weeks, a lawyer from New Jersey, made it a threesome.

I traveled all over the country campaigning, and when I

arrived in Detroit, sure enough, I led the election. However, I did not get fifty percent of the votes which resulted in the first run-off ever in the history of the NBA. This was in 1981 when I became its president. My stated campaign goals and priorities were:

- Render effective and supportive service and leadership during my one-year tenure as President-Elect. Also, I would prepare to insure a continuity of leadership, programs, and priorities.

- Provide strong leadership that makes clear our willingness to cooperate on matters of mutual concern with other Bar Associations, including the American Bar Association (ABA), but also to make equally clear our unwillingness, indeed our collective commitment, to preserve this Association's historical purpose, intendments, and raison d'etre. To be sure, our original reason for existence has never changed. This message must go forth and be repeated to the entire legal community of this nation, and to the extent necessary, even our own members would do well to be reminded.

- Reorganize and place enhanced emphasis on the membership effort. This fundamentally important effort should be decentralized primarily shouldered by the local affiliate under increased supervision by the Regional Director. The single most important problem with our membership effort, and our financial condition, is there are simply too many lawyers who are members of our affiliates who have not joined or financially support the NBA.

- Establish a dues structure that contemplates local affiliate accountability for each lawyer in its jurisdiction.

This approach would qualify each lawyer for, but would not fully discharge the individual dues obligation to the NBA.

• Increase NBA services, particularly communication with our membership, and make a better effort at realizing the financial benefit that can be derived for the NBA in the provision of membership services.

• Develop and implement a fiscal program that provides first for the maintenance of a national staff sufficient in size to meet our in-house program and service needs. This we must do for ourselves. Second, such fiscal program would include private and governmental grants and contracts, but only if they are cost-efficient as well as income-producing for the NBA.

• Seek to initiate client relations for our members and explore financial support for this Association from States and private entities in the international community, particularly in Africa and the Third World.

• Endeavor, with minimum cost to this Association, to promote and disseminate more fully the public relations story (past, present, and future) of the NBA and the Black Lawyers in America. There has not been enough said; thus, not enough people know what we have done, are doing, or can for the people of this nation or for black people particularly in the private delivery of legal services.

• Work diligently to make the black lawyer in private practice and the black Lawyer just entering the profession more attractive to each other. The accomplishment of this goal will foster more Black law firms and will, I believe, be in the long run in the best interest of black lawyers generally.

• Make it clear to the nation, and particularly to those involved in the appointive and confirmation process, that we need and must have more black judges in the Federal judiciary. There remain circuits, multiple district states and many individual districts in which no, or too few black judges sit. In this regard, we must maintain and enhance our capacity to participate in the evaluation of judicial nominees. Where possible, we must seek the appointment and assist in the election and re-election of State judges.

James Cobb, Dennis Archer, Chesterfield Smith, Warren Hope Dawson - Washington, DC, 1983 at National Bar Association's Annual Dinner

- Promote unity among the membership of this Association so that we can proceed, without division among ourselves, to perform the many tasks that require our collective attention and best effort.

- Dedicate myself to a community of leadership concept which contemplates that every effort should be made to continue and follow through on worthy programs, goals, and promises of the preceding administration.

The convention that I presided over as president of the NBA was in Seattle, Washington. Among my invited quests were Harold Washington, the first black mayor of Chicago, the mayor's corporation's counsel, James D. Montgomery and Jane Kennedy, a NFL television personality.

- During my tenure, I traveled extensively telling the story: "Black lawyers still face vestiges of racial prejudice; President Ronald Reagan wasn't appointing blacks to federal judgeships in the numbers he should have; blacks remained at a disadvantage in the political arena." The impact of my efforts is still being felt.

- I led, and spoke on behalf of, twelve thousand plus black lawyers, judges and law students and was the first from Tampa and second from Florida to ever do so.

Warren Hope Dawson, as 40th President of the NBA, produced the inaugural issue of the National Bar Association Magazine.

First of its kind! Ever!

- True to a campaign promise, I Founded the NBA Magazine. The NBA magazine served the crucial need to inform black lawyers and others of the accomplishments and contributions of African Americans in the law and articulating outreach during my official travels. I now serve as Honorary Editor-In-Chief of the magazine and board member along with Suhuyini Abudulai, Christal Edwards, Debra Hatter, Sheryl Montour, Frank Motley, Jonathan Richardson, and Freida L. Wheaton.

- Convened a "Summit of Black Lawyers."

- Inaugurated the Chesterfield Smith Award

- Appointed a black woman, Marilyn Holyfield, as a delegate to the A.B.A. House of Delegates.

- Accepted the sage advice and was guided by the keen insight of John Crump, Esquire, the long serving Executive Director of the National Bar Association. Could not have done it without him.

In 1983, during the National Bar Association's annual meeting held in Seattle, Washington, I as president of the Association, spoke out against the death of an incarcerated black man. The hangman's noose had been replaced by police choke holds. A debate, regarding the use of choke holds by jail officials, led to new measures with limitations being put on the practice.

In 2014, Eric Garner died in Staten Island, New York, after a police officer put him in what has been described as a "choke hold" for about fifteen to nineteen minutes.

"I can't breathe" became a national rally cry during approximately fifty demonstrations around the country. Using a choke hold was against New York police policy, but apparently, they abandoned the policy. Things were changing for Garner's family as they were awarded $5.9 Million in an out of court settlement.

In 2020, with the death of George Floyd, the world discovered that the choke hold had been replaced by policemen kneeling on the "suspect's" neck.

Both my campaign and service earned the attention of some rather notable people:

> *"Congratulations for a very successful year. I was pleased to see the National Bar Association surpass its goals under your leadership raising its already high standards of prominence and influence."*
>
> *Walter F. Mondale*

Summit Of Black Lawyers in America, March 1983
Leon Higginbothom, Vernon A. Jordon, Warren Hope Dawson & Maynard Jackson

Andrew Young, Warren Hope Dawson and Rev. Jessie Jackson

"Today we congratulate you upon the outstanding leadership you have given to the National Bar Association. Your creative talent and innovative programs have given the National Bar Association a visibility which has enhanced the cause of justice among blacks and other Americans. Your active "participation in the Operation Push Southern Crusade for voter registration and enforcement of the Voting Rights Act evidenced by outstanding legal skills and determinative strategies for litigation on behalf of the voiceless is turning new pages in the Nation's history and writing a whole litany of new social conveyance for all Americans".

--Reverend Jesse Jackson,
National President
Operation Push

1979 Meeting of Black Lawyers of Florida on the steps of the Supreme Court
Row 1: Rodney Gregory, Anna Motter, Doris Jenkins, Isaac Williams, Shirley Walker, Frank Scruggs, Walter Kelly, Robert Collins, Warren Hope Dawson
Row 2: Robert Travis, Theodore Bowers, Luther Smith, Eddie Rogers, Bishop Holifield, Larry White, Morris Milton, Thomas Stringer
Row 3: Jack McLean, William Stevens, Roosevelt Randolph, Alfred Washington
Row 4: Isaac Nunn, unknown, unknown, Henry Latimer, unknown, Joseph Morrell

of Florida – Warren Hope Dawson, President
Row 1: Horace Hill, Wilkie Ferguson, William Hutchinson, Henry Hunter, Emerson Thompson, H.T. Smith, Perry Little, Marva Davis, unknown, Margaret Ben
Row 2: Algie Cooper, Harold Knowles, Martin Black, John Marks, Carolyn House, unknown, Danny Watts
Row 3: Rickie Williams, Robert Morrison, Leon Rolle, Unknown, Ralph Armstead, Zebedee Wright
Row 5: William Johnson, J Blayne Jennings, Reese Marshall, Johnny Mahan

Chapter 6

A 27 Year Battle

My contribution to the struggle for fair and equal education for all public-school students of Hillsborough County, Florida, was a twenty-seven-year journey. To fully understand my role, consider that it was part of a continuum that began in December of 1958. This school desegregation litigation in the Federal Courts followed the historic decision in the case of <u>Brown v. Board of Education,</u> 347 U.S. 483 (1954) of Topeka, Kansas, decided May 17, 1954, by the Supreme Court of the United States. The Hillsborough case became known as Manning vs. the School Board of Hillsborough County.

The Hillsborough School District was and is one of the largest school districts in the nation – and still growing. For example, by the year 2014, the District had some two hundred and eighty schools serving over 200,500 (211,731 by 2015) students. There were one hundred forty two elementary schools, forty three middle schools, twenty seven high schools, three K-8, four career centers, nine exceptional centers, four HiTECs, and forty seven charter schools. This district, like all the school districts in Florida, is co-terminus with the geography of the county – and that in part accounts for the large school districts in Florida. Regarding Hillsborough County, in 2014 the county population demographics was: Asian - 3.68%; African American - 21.40%; Hispanic - 32.02%; Indian - .22%; Multi - 5.38%; and Caucasian – 37.30%. In 2015, the county was projected to have a population of 1,349,050, making it the fourth most populous county in the state. In land area, the county covers a massive twelve hundred sixty six square miles – an important consideration on the issue of busing to achieve desegregation.

Robert Saunders, Warren Hope Dawson, Ann Porter, Elaine Jones, Andrew Manning.

The Manning lawsuit was originally filed by Attorney Francisco Rodriguez, an Afro-Cuban American lawyer, who many regarded as the number one civil rights lawyer in Florida during the 1950s and 1960s. Mr. Rodriquez brought the case on behalf of certain named plaintiffs and their children. Those Plaintiffs were: Andrew L. Manning, by his father and next friend, Willie M. Manning, Shayron B. Reed and Sandra B. Reed by their father and next friend, Sandra B. Reed, Nathaniel Cannon, Norman Thomas Cannon, Tyrone Cannon, Darrel Cannon, by their father and next friend, Nathaniel Cannon, Sr., Renee Myers, by her father and next friend, Randolph Myers. While there were named plaintiffs, this case was actually a Class Action suit brought by those plaintiffs on behalf of all Negro children and their parents who lived in the

Hillsborough School District.

A distinguished list of lawyers from the NAACP Legal Defense and Education Fund, including Thurgood Marshall, Constance Baker Motley, Julius Chambers, Elaine Jones, Norman Chachkin and, Victor Bolden joined and contributed greatly to the litigation of the Manning case.

Between the years of 1958 and 1971 (some thirteen years), the Hillsborough County School Board reluctantly promised and ultimately failed to achieve meaningful desegregation of the public schools. The initial promise or plan was the School Board would desegregate the schools using a process called "one-grade-a-year," beginning with first grade. When it was later determined the one-grade-a-year plan was not working and would take too long, even if implemented, the School Board then offered to desegregate based on "a pairing plan." That plan contemplated taking a historically black school and pairing it with a historically white school. The two schools that were "paired" would then achieve racial desegregation by sharing or exchanging portions of their student body. After some years of that pairing plan, it became apparent, it too was not effectively desegregating the schools. A "majority-to-minority transfer plan" was but another failed plan undertaken by the School Board.

One excuse for some of the desegregation plan failures during the 1958-1971 time frame was racially segregated housing. That problem challenged School Districts to utilize busing to overcome the problem.

1971 – Krentzman Decision

Between 1958 and 1970, it would be fair to characterize the school desegregation efforts as slow to none.

In 1971, the U.S. Supreme Court ruled in the case of Swann v. Charlotte-Mecklenburg Board of Education, 402 U.S. 1 (1971), that busing was a legitimate tool to facilitate the desegregation of public schools, particularly in those instances where segregated housing was frustrating the desegregation process. Because of the ruling in Swann, the Honorable Ben Krentzman, the then presiding judge in the Manning case ordered, without a request from either party, that the Hillsborough County School Board promptly submit a new plan of desegregation utilizing busing. Also in that Order, Judge Krentzman instituted a plan to dis-establish the historically black high schools: Middleton, Blake, and Marshall, as sixth and seventh grade centers.

1971 – Busing

While I sincerely did not believe that it was Krentzman's purpose, or intent to punish the black community, his 1971 decision nevertheless caused black families to bear a disproportional share of the hardship and inconvenience caused by the approved busing plan. It is more likely that his plan reflected frustration with the School Board's desegregation pace.

The approved plan contemplated a ratio in each school

to approximate an 80/20 ratio (white-black). To achieve that ratio, busing, considerable busing, was necessary. Again, the brunt of the busing burden fell squarely on the shoulders of young black children who were bused to remote schools ten of their twelve school years. While slightly older white children were bused only two years out of their twelve school years.

One memorable example of the disproportionate burden: the black children from a two to three block area of the College Hill Housing Project attended twelve different grade schools.

Even though the burden for white children was significantly lighter, there was nevertheless a greater hue and cry from the white community over this matter of "forced busing" – their term. Among their arguments against busing was it needlessly consumed precious gasoline during a fuel crisis. I publicly responded by pointing out that at gas guzzling stock car races, enough gas is spilled on the ground to bus several loads of children to a school where they can get a quality and equal education.

In 1970, the then Federal Fifth Circuit Court of Appeals examined whether the HCSB had sufficiently eradicated the illegal dual school system such that it could be found "unitary." Relying upon the six "so-called" Green Factors. That Court, then based in New Orleans, Louisiana, concluded that regarding three factors (transportation, extracurricular activities, and facilities), Hillsborough had indeed achieved a unitary school district.

However, based on its examination of three other factors (faculty desegregation, staff desegregation, and student assignments), the court found HCSB had fallen short and had not attained unitary status. The case was then sent back to the Federal District Court in Tampa with instructions for the Tampa Court to remedy the deficiencies.

In 1971, the United States Supreme Court, in the case of Swann vs. Charlotte-Mecklenburg Board of Education, gave firm guidance to a Federal Court in Tampa (and other district courts) on its equitable powers to remedy illegal segregation, including busing. On May 11, 1971, just 21 days after Swann was decided, the Tampa Federal Court directed the HCSB to submit a comprehensive desegregation plan that conformed with the requirements of Swann. A plan was submitted and approved by the Court in an order dated July 2, 1971 (the "July 1971 Order").

In 1991, the School Board lawyers and I, as counsel for the plaintiff class, entered a consent decree (1991 Consent Order). The primary reason for the 1991 Consent Order was to enable HCSB to reorganize the school district, to eliminate single grade centers and to create middle schools. The 1991 Consent Order, which was to be implemented over a 7-year period, did not annul the July 1971 Order, but merely modified it.

In 1994, I, along with other Civil Rights lawyers from the NAACP Legal Defense and Education Fund, moved to enforce the 1991 Consent Order. The matter was referred to a magistrate judge who recommended denying the motion. The district judge, however, deferred ruling on the motion and sua sponte recommitted the matter to the magistrate judge to consider whether the school district had become unitary, thereby removing the need for continued federal judicial oversight.

In October of 1996, the magistrate judge conducted a

7-day hearing, at which both sides presented considerable evidence. In August of 1997, the magistrate judge issued a detailed report where she recommended the district court find that HCSB had achieved unitary status and thus should be released from federal judicial supervision. Without holding an evidentiary hearing, the district judge in a 110-page order dated October 26, 1998, rejected in part and adopted in part the magistrate judge's report and recommendation. The district judge concluded that HCSB had not attained unitary status and therefore, federal judicial supervision was still warranted.

Within ten days of the order, dated October 26, 1998, HCSB lawyers filed a motion to alter or amend the judgment. The district court, in a 13-page order, denied the motion on December 4, 1998. HCSB lawyers then filed an appeal to the Federal Eleventh Circuit Court of Appeals based in Atlanta, Georgia.

On March 16, 2001, after oral argument in Atlanta, the court of appeals affirmed the decision of the magistrate judge, i.e., that HCSB had attained unitary status and no longer required Federal Judicial supervision. On October 1, 2001, the Supreme Court of the United States denied further review of the matter – thus ending the forty-three-year legal saga through which this School District was pushed to eliminate racially segregated public schools in Tampa, Hillsborough County, Florida.

Attorney's Fees in the Manning Case

As previously indicated, I first entered the Manning Case in 1973 or 1974 as a cooperating attorney for the NAACP Legal Defense and Education Fund, Inc.(LDF), a civil rights law firm based in New York City is different from, and not the same as the National Association for the Advancement of Colored People (NAACP), a civil rights organization based in Baltimore.

While the lawyers representing the School Board were being paid every thirty days during the forty-three years that this legal saga was in the courts, I received no fees until near the end. When I first raised the matter of the School Board paying attorney fees to me, and to the other lawyers who had represented the plaintiffs, the suggestion was a laughing matter to at least one of the lawyers for the School Board. I had only asked, "Aren't we supposed to be paid something for all this legal work we've done for all these years?" The answer was, "Show the documentation." So, utilizing the voluminous court files that had accumulated over the years, I took on the task to recreate, blow by blow, the legal work done in that 43-year-old case. With the help of my friend and mentor, William Reece Smith, Jr., we were ultimately awarded attorney's fees for the legal work of lawyers from LDF, including yours truly. I saw to it that the widow of Francisco Rodriguez and the family of James Sanderlin were remembered in the distribution of that belated and nominal fee award.

♪ *"I shall not - I shall not be moved*
Just like a tree that's planted by the water
I shall not be moved" ♪

It is completely fair and accurate that my legal career could be defined by work in the Manning case. My work in that matter is certainly my ticket to claim to be a civil rights lawyer. While ostensibly, I represented a class of plaintiffs described as all Negro children and their parents, it was and is my belief that this case was really all about an equal educational opportunity for all of the children, black, white, etc., in this very large and very diverse public school district. I enjoyed the work I did in this case and willingly embrace the fact that my legal work has already benefited thousands of children of all races – and countless millions in years to come.

In all fairness, the gracious decision of the Hillsborough County School Board on January 17, 2017, to honor me by dedicating a new school in my name, made it all worthwhile.

The Warren Hope Dawson Elementary School

Location: 12961 Boggy Creek Drive,
          Riverview, FL 33579

Cost to Construct: $20-million
Opening Date: Thursday, August 10, 2017
Dedication Date: Saturday, April 28, 2018
Grades Levels: Pre-K - 5th
Pupil Capacity: 950
Mascot: The Dawson Dragons
Colors: Grey & Dark Blue

Motto:
Providing "HOPE" for our future, one child at a time.

Chapter 7

Legendary Fights

Quote from "Confidence has Driven Dawson": "Had I done those and some other things I would have done in 1966 through 1972, frankly, I would have been killed. Just my air and demeanor probably would have gotten me killed in 1966." WHD

Awkward But Legal

As previously indicated, I actively recruited Bobby Thompson, a native Tampanian, and former popular athlete, to become a candidate for City Clerk of the City of Tampa. In the early '70s, the city clerk position was an elected office. Without demeaning that position, it is fair to say that for that reason, it was my thought that the office of city clerk was a good place for the black community to start.

Among other things, I was his campaign treasurer and had donated Thompson's qualifying fee. That donation was public information, and it didn't take long for my involvement to be reported by the media.

When the incumbent, Bill Stark, learned of my support of Thompson, he was very upset. In fact, one local newspaper reported he was "shook up" about my asserting my personal rights as a private citizen.

Stark protested that I, as an assistant city attorney and city employee, should not have participated in a campaign against my employer. I agreed and informed him that while I had some duty to him, as the city clerk, I owed no duty to him as a candidate for reelection. City Attorney William Reece Smith, Jr., agreed with me, and so did the media. In this regard, a media comment was that my conduct might have been awkward, but it was legal.

Dawson vs Goliath

In March 1973, in an effort to launch a limousine service, I waged war against Greyhound Lines, Inc., Yellow Cab of Tampa, Diamond Cab Co, Southern Tours, Gulf Coast Motor Lines, Inc. and Florida Limousine Service before the Florida Public Service Commission. I won. Greyhound appealed my Commission victory to the Florida Supreme Court, and I won again.

I wanted to operate in Hillsborough, Pasco, Pinellas, and Polk counties. I was offering a VIP limousine service from those counties to anywhere in Florida, especially to popular vacation spots like Disney World and Cypress Gardens. The service was also ideal for funeral homes, weddings, civic organizations and private businesses.

In this regard, broad community support aided my victories. Among the community leaders who backed my efforts were: Rev. W. H. Gordon of College Hill Baptist Church and Rev. H. McDonald Nelson of Allen Temple A.M.E. Church.

Unfortunately, my victories were wiped out by a nationwide gasoline shortage that held sway for several months. So much for an excellent entrepreneurial idea that was ahead of its time.

They All Look Alike

A legendary battle of significant proportion occurred in the court system in Bartow, Florida, the county seat of the infamous "imperial" Polk County, Florida. I had been engaged to represent a young black man accused of assaulting an elderly white man in the parking area of a local mall. It was in the middle of July 1980, a blistering time of the year and a bit hot in the courtroom as well.

I asked Jeffery Streeter, a 19-year-old, young black man, from Haines City, who just happened to be in the courthouse hallway, to portray Lee Marvin Anderson (my actual client) during a trial where the identity of the black defendant was very much in question.

Streeter sat quietly at the defense table with me, as three "eyewitnesses" identified him as the assailant. I asked no questions of the State's witnesses, and when the State rested, I immediately asked the judge to dismiss the case against Anderson. Judge Edward Threadgill, Jr. summarily denied the motion. When I attempted to make clear that the real defendant (Anderson) was seated in the court room but not at counsel's table, the judge ignored my efforts and proceeded to find Streeter guilty and directed that he be taken into custody.

While my own liberty was placed in question, by an Order to Show Cause why I should not be "held in contempt of court" for having a person other than the defendant to sit with me at counsel's table, I was much more concerned about Streeter's loss of his liberty. With the assistance of Attorney Larry Jackson, a Lakeland practitioner, Streeter was released from jail. With the assistance of James Kynes, a previous Florida Attorney General, David Shear, a previous president of The Florida Bar, Crosby Few, a Tampa practitioner and previous law school roommate of Judge Threadgill, a Holland & Knight lawyer, and Tom McDonald, an acknowledged guru on lawyer ethics, my liberty was vigorously defended and joyously preserved.

Media coverage of this Bartow, Florida episode was carried across the nation.

The Richard Kelly Stories

As I reflect on cases I either had or knew about, I am moved to share a "story" that did not directly involve me, and yet indirectly it did.

In 2014, I had a case in Dade City, Pasco County, Florida that required three hearings in two days. Coincidentally, all three hearings were scheduled before two white female judges. To put it mildly, I was treated very, very rough by both judges. That treatment brought back unpleasant memories of the Dade City I had heard of and came to know very early in my legal career.

In particular, I was prompted to recall a legendary "story" of Judge Richard Kelly, who had been a lawyer practicing in Pasco County in his early days. At one time, he was the city attorney for the small town of Zephyrhills, Florida, and at some point, served as an Assistant United States Attorney for the Middle District of Florida. Kelly later became a state circuit judge sitting primarily in Dade City at a time when it was a sleepy little town that could be fairly described as segregated and racist.

I do not recall if I ever personally appeared before Judge Kelly, but the "story" they tell is that Judge Kelly presided over a rape trial of a black man charged with raping a white woman. It might be helpful to note that during that time, a black man convicted of raping a white woman meant almost certain death in the electric chair.

The "story" continues: On that particular Monday morning at 9:00 a.m., Judge Kelly came to his court room dead set on quickly wrapping up the case of this black man. Judge Kelly had decided he was going to basically push this man into pleading guilty to the charge and thus avoid a full-blown trial before a jury. So, rather than bringing in the jury at 9:00 a.m., he allegedly said to this defendant, "Now boy, you know you're guilty. I don't know why you would want to put these white folks to all this trouble of going through a trial when you know you're guilty. Now, so why don't you just plead guilty to this charge and get this over with?" - or words to that affect. He repeatedly asked the defendant whether he was willing to change his plea to guilty - and the young man kept saying "no" because he wasn't guilty.

Well, Kelly was determined to coerce this man and to have him plead guilty, so the process went on well into late morning. It was almost noon, and Kelly still hadn't brought in the jury. He kept talking to this young man telling him in words to this effect; "I don't know why you would put these white folks through all this trouble. They've got things they need to do other than giving you a trial here on something you know you did." The young man still refused to plead guilty.

The "story" continues: At twelve noon and time for lunch, Kelly having verbally beaten up on this young man all morning, still wouldn't start the trial. Kelly told him, as they broke for lunch, "Now, you got a good lawyer sitting there with you. You need to talk to that lawyer and come back in here and do the right thing. Okay, you go take a break now." The young man was encouraged to plead guilty, though innocent, to at least be sentenced to life in prison and thus avoid the electric chair.

When he returned from lunch, Kelly again inquired of the young man, "How do you plead to this charge? Have you changed your mind and are you're willing to plead guilty? The young man finally said, "Yes, I plead guilty." Judge Kelly said, "I direct you to continue standing right where you are." "... And it is the judgment and sentence of this court that you die in the electric chair. Next case!"

While the forgoing "story" is legendary and is probably a mixture of facts, exaggerations, recalls and add-ons, the following story, which also involves Judge Kelly, is largely documented in news and court papers.

Later in the 1970s, Judge Kelly, ran for and was elected to the Congress of the United States. After a few years in Congress, the FBI suspicioned that there were some congressmen in Washington, DC willing to take bribes from people from Arab nations. So, the FBI set up a sting called "Abscam."

Sure enough, Richard Kelly was among the congressmen believed to be involved in the bribery activity. To be sure, the FBI arranged a meeting for Kelly in a room at a Washington, DC hotel. There, Kelly met with undercover agents posing as Arabs. With cameras rolling behind a curtain, the agents offered Kelly twenty five thousand dollars, as the first part of a fifty thousand dollar payoff, for him to vote favorably on certain legislation then pending before Congress. Kelly accepted the money and was later arrested and charged with taking a bribe.

When Kelly was released from jail, a television crew approached him for an interview. They asked, "Congressman, what do you have to say about this arrest? They arrested and charged you with accepting a bribe in this thing they called Abscam. Do you have anything to say?" Kelly took an interesting approach and replied, "I was conducting my own investigation. I knew they were up to something, and so I was conducting my own investigation. I went into that room, they handed me that money, and I took it." Illustrating his actions while the cameras were rolling, he said, "I took that money, you see, I put it right in my pocket, and I said to myself, now I know I got them." A news person said, "Sir, with all due respect, you say you know you got them, but they say they know they got you."

Kelly was caused to stand trial before a judge and jury in Washington, DC. The jury convicted Kelly of taking a bribe. However, the trial judge set aside the jury verdict and wrote a thirty-seven-page opinion in which he concluded the government had entrapped Kelly.

The trial judge involved was U.S. District Judge William Vincent Bryant, who at the time was also the chief judge of the district court in Washington, DC. The judiciary in Washington was diverse and included women, blacks, and other minorities. Judge Bryant was black, a graduate of Howard Law School, and number one in his class. He had been the first black assistant U.S. attorney in the District of

Columbia. I am positive Judge Bryant had no idea of what this Richard Kelly had done to that poor black man down in Dade City, Florida. I am also persuaded that it would not have mattered. Judge Bryant was eminently fair - even to Richard Kelly.

As Paul Harvey, the renowned radio newsman used to say, "Now, for the rest of the story."

The government decided to exercise its right to appeal Judge Bryant's decision to give this Dade City fellow the break-of-his-life. The appeal was made to a three-judge panel of the U.S. Court of Appeals for the District of Columbia. On review, District Judge Bryant's decision was reversed, and the guilty verdict was reinstated. Interestingly, it was another black judge, Spottswood William Robinson, III, a Howard law graduate, a former Dean of the Howard Law School, who at the time was also the chief judge of the Appellate Court in Washington, DC, who wrote the opinion reinstating the guilty verdict. While Kelly was sent to prison, he was clearly treated fairly by the black judges in Washington.

The treatment I received in 2014 in Dade City, Florida had a racial odor to it and caused me to give fresh recollection to the "stories" of Richard Kelly. Frankly, the treatment was somewhat surprising given that some diversity (women) had finally arrived in the ranks of the judiciary in Dade City, Florida.

The Nathaniel Sanders Case

One of my more memorable cases involved an incident on Highway 37, between Mulberry and Lakeland, Florida, in a community known as Medulla.

It happened sometime in January or February of 1979, and involved young black men engaged in a common small-town cold-weather, nighttime socialization activity – they would gather old automobile tires, set them on fire and stand around for hours shooting the breeze. This was a great way to socialize and keep warm outdoors on chilly nights.

On the night in question, there were fifteen to twenty young fellows, between the ages of seventeen to twenty eight, standing around the fire talking when one of them decided to drive his old four-door sedan up South Florida Avenue to a 7-11 to get some beer. Six other fellows got in the car and joined him.

Once at the 7-11, four of them went into the store where one of them, unbeknownst to the other three, quickly decided to shoplift a six-pack of beer. As he (Robert) exited the store, without paying for the beer, the store manager, who was seated in a car also parked in front of the store, confronted Robert shouting that he had not paid for the beer and ordered him to take it back into the store. Robert obediently took the beer back and then reemerged from the store. The manager then confronted Robert, hit him with the blackjack and moments later, shot him with a pistol. All of the manager's violent actions towards Robert occurred in plain view of the three young men who had remained in the car. Nathaniel, my client, was one of them.

As they say, "The Lord don't like ugly, and somebody is always watching." So, Nathaniel jumped out of the car and ran up to the store manager, who still had the smoking gun in his hand, and swiftly made an athletic move. It must have appeared to the manager he was moving in one direction when, in fact, he was moving in another direction. In the process, Nathaniel knocked the gun out of the manager's hand. With the gun on the ground, it was a matter of whether Nathaniel or the manager was going to get it back. As it turned out, Nathaniel was the size of a football defensive back. He was not large, in terms size, but had strong arms and was very fast. In nothing flat, Nathaniel had picked up the gun.

Up to this point, the manager had been the "hunter" and Robert had been "the game." Suddenly, the manager found himself in the position of being "the game," and Nathaniel had become "the hunter." Whereupon, the manager took off running down the sidewalk. Nathaniel gave chase and fired the pistol four times at the manager, as they were running.

About fifty yards down the sidewalk, the manager fell. The police reported, Nathaniel came up to him after he had fallen and shot him in the temple, while he was on the ground. Actually, all four shots had hit the manager and caused him to fall. This point makes the difference between being a first-degree or second-degree murder charge. Afraid, Nathaniel ran away.

Because of what the police thought had happened, they charged Nathaniel with first-degree murder. He was also at large, and no one knew where he was. His family came to me because we had been family friends for years. They were aware of the media coverage that described this incident as one in which a white manager had been shot three times in the back and once in the temple by this young black man. The family feared the police would find him and kill him, rather than bring him back to justice. If Nathaniel managed to come back alive, they wanted me to represent him. I agreed.

Approximately six months later, Nathaniel was apprehended somewhere in the Fort Lauderdale, Florida area. The local media exploited this situation to the fullest.

The case was assigned to Judge Love, probably one of the nicer judges of the time. Nevertheless, because of the level and tone of the publicity, I thought I could use some help and arranged for a couple of young lawyers from a major law firm to assist me.

In Florida, a grand jury is used to charge, not to determine guilt or innocence, only to determine the charge based purely on the information provided by the prosecutor. Defense attorneys are not allowed to present information. In many counties, there are two times per year a grand jury listens to prosecutors and decide if there is sufficient information to charge defendants with first-degree murder.

For a capital offense, where the death penalty could ultimately be given, they use the grand jury to indict. Nathaniel's case came before a grand jury, and he was indeed charged with first-degree murder.

I set out to attack the indictment. I knew full well there had been very few blacks, if any, who had served on the Grand Jury for the state circuit that included Polk County.

Likewise, I was absolutely positive that no black person had ever been selected to serve as the Grand Jury foreman in this county.

Around the same time, the Supreme Court of the United States decided the case of <u>Rose v. Mitchell</u>, 443 U.S. 545, 1979. The underline Rose case held that an indictment would have to fall if there had been racial discrimination in selecting the Grand Jury foreman, particularly if it was shown that there had been a pattern of discrimination over a period of years. This Tennessee case presented a thirty plus year pattern of discrimination.

I was sure, in the previous thirty five years, there had not been a black person picked as a grand jury foreman in Polk County. So, I set out to attack the indictment based on discrimination. I was certain I could prove it. I asked Judge Love to order the clerk to gather the records for 35 years and provide the names of everyone who had served on the Grand Jury and especially those who had served as foreman. That meant reviewing the roles of about seventy separate grand juries.

I then asked the judge to order the supervisor of elections, the only governmental entity then authorized to collect and maintain information regarding race, to identify each person who had served on a grand jury - by race.

In Florida, Circuit judges rotate the duty of convening the Grand Jury and among the duties of the convening judge is the responsibility to pick the Grand Jury foreman. Of course this is different from the process by which a foreman of a trial jury is selected. Fellow jurors pick the foreman of a trial jury.

You can imagine that the local media was covering every aspect of this intended attack on the racially discriminatory process by which grand jury foremen had been selected over the past thirty five years. Due in part to the media coverage, the games began. What games? The first situation involved the deputy clerk who had been given the responsibility to locate and produce the Grand Jury rolls during the previous thirty five years.

From what I recall, the deputy clerk was a young white male about twenty five years old. A reporter, who was also a young white male, from the Lakeland Ledger newspaper came over, at my request, and asked the clerk how he was doing. The clerk said he was doing the best he could to get it done. He then went on to say, "if those jungle bunnies would register to vote", he wouldn't have the problem he was having.

I am sure the young deputy felt comfortable talking to this young reporter, given their common age and race. The deputy clerk had a misguided sense of security. His comfort level was misguided because the reporter had an office directly across from the courthouse in Bartow.

The reporter went right back across the street and wrote a story and fully quoted what this young deputy clerk had said. It was all over the news in a big way. The white Clerk of Court was a man named Dud Dixon who happened to be from Mulberry, my hometown, and who knew of me. It embarrassed him so much he suspended the young deputy clerk.

During a hearing, I advanced a legal theory that was not as specious as it may sound. I moved to squash the indictment and argued that Nathaniel was in a situation where he had personally watched a violent felony occur in his presence (when the manager shot Robert), and the felon tried to flee. Those facts, I further argued, were not dissimilar to a scenario in which Nathaniel had observed the daughter of the president of a local country club being attacked and raped – and the perpetrator was shot by Nathaniel during his attempt to escape.

Those facts, I suggested, would have labeled Nathaniel a hero at a dinner at the club in his honor. Judge Love very quickly asked if I had anything else to say. I said, "No sir." He then promptly denied the motion. I wasn't surprised. Again, the details of my argument were all over the newspapers.

Later in the litigation, Judge Love counseled me from the bench that I was delaying the case, and if I persisted, he was going to have to put me in jail. I responded, "This case is not about me," and asked if what he really wanted to do was put me in jail. Again, the newspapers picked up the exchange and gave it more coverage than it deserved.

My next move was to do something almost unthinkable for an attorney. I subpoenaed every circuit judge, including all retired judges except Judge Love (since he was presiding), to testify in the case. The prevailing comment from lawyers was: "Wow, they are going to bury you." I was undeterred and was ultimately successful in getting the indictment dismissed.

Of course, the case did not end there; a new grand jury was quickly convened with a black woman selected as foreman. Historically, the first black person ever named foreman of a grand jury in Polk County, Florida. This new grand jury promptly re-indicted Nathaniel.

In defense of Nathaniel, I had put the system on trial and forced a disposition that avoided a death sentence. Nathaniel pled to second-degree murder, served eleven years in prison, and was released.

Ye Mystic Krewe of Gasparilla

Undoubtedly, the biggest and most successful effort to bring diversity to Tampa and Hillsborough County Florida occurred during the 1990 - 1991 revolt against the Ye Mystic Krewe of Gasparilla. It was all about the XXV Super Bowl of the National Football League (NFL) coming to town, and the opportunity that event presented to expose the lack of diversity at many levels in the "Tampa Bay" community.

Tampa, like many major cities in the nation, has a local annual celebration designed to energize the community, much like New Orleans' Mardi Gras and Savannah's St Patrick's Day. In Tampa, it is Gasparilla, which began around 1904. It involves a large fleet of "pirate ships" participating in a water invasion. The Hillsborough River is saturated with elaborately decorated watercraft of all types. The invasion ends with the Mayor surrendering the key to the city to pirates, who then celebrate their victory, viewed by thousands, with a street parade of simulated pirate ships and their crews. The original organizers called themselves "Ye Mystic Krewe." Membership included no blacks or women. This celebration of a mythical pirate (Jose Gaspar) was and continues to be, essential to the Tampa Bay area's revenue stream.

Planning for the 1991 Gasparilla celebration was electrified by the NFL's decision to bring the Super Bowl to Tampa. In particular, in a joint presentation, the Krewe and the NFL proposed that ABC Wide World of Sports televise the pirate water invasion and Gasparilla street parade on Saturday, and then the 1991 Super Bowl on Sunday.

My band of rebels and I took the position that this racially segregated event should not be televised, and ABC nor any other network should carry it. We demanded that the NFL not allow it to happen. We had numerous meetings for about a year; we met with the City, ABC, and the NFL. Finally, it was agreed that this non-diverse event should not be publicized to the world.

Understandably, the Krewe was furious. We (black people) were interfering with an uninterrupted, ninety-five-year tradition by demanding, among other things, that blacks be permitted to join the Ye Mystic Krewe. The Krewe's role in promoting tourism, visiting children and veterans in hospitals, raising money for the Salvation Army, their annual debutante and coronation balls were all about white male privilege.

The captain of the Krewe and most of its members decided to cancel Gasparilla rather than allow blacks to join the Krewe. Another event (called Bomboleo) was hastily put together to fill the gap.

Our group, the Coalition of African American Organizations, made written demands of Ye Mystic Krewe of Gasparilla that were aimed at reversing as many social injustices, in as many places, and in as many local institutions as possible. We fully understood this was clearly the most opportune time to force the hand of the community's power structure.

This revolt resulted in a more diverse Tampa. For the first time, African Americans, Latinos, women and other ethnic groups were admitted to membership in previously all-white male organizations and positions. Including the likes of the Yacht Club and the University Club. Corporate Boards of many of the major banks and utility companies like General Telephone and Tampa Electric; and yes, the Mystic Krewe eventually took in a few black members. In turn, the Krewe began to finance other units and groups, including women and Latino, so that they could participate in Gasparilla.

Our efforts also motivated the NFL to create a format for addressing future minority participation as it moves the Super Bowl from city to city.

During that first Tampa hosted Super Bowl, the mayors of both cities (The then Washington Redskins and the then Los Angeles Raiders) just happened to be African American. I had to enlist the help of a white lawyer friend, James Thompson, who at my request, invited the then Mayor of Washington, DC, Marion Barry, who was in town for the game to dine at the University Club.

Thompson made the reservation, paid the tab using his membership number, and declined reimbursement. Fortunately, there were some white men of good will around like Thompson. However, Tampa at the time was simply not ready to be a genuine host to an event as diverse as the Super Bowl. It was an embarrassment to me and to the City of Tampa.

Without apology, my efforts were personal, but not for my personal benefit. For that reason, my personal ethics suggested that I should not seek to be a member of the

Krewe or to otherwise gain personally from the concessions achieved. For that reason, it was nearly fifteen years later, before I joined the University Club.

If, at some future date, someone undertook to search the annals of Tampa and Hillsborough County Florida to determine when, if ever, the Tampa community took well-defined steps to assure justice and equality to all of its citizens, they may find the answer involved the revolt against Ye Mystic Krewe of Gasparilla in 1990 - 1991, a campaign that I am proud to have led.

Why the Whydah?

My two-year battle with Silver Screen Entertainment directors, (Tom Bernstein and Roland Betts) and the City of Tampa over a former slave ship called the Whydah, began in 1991 with a personal phone call from Federal Magistrate Judge Joyce London Alexander from Boston, Massachusetts.

Judge Alexander called to say, "Warren, I see from the New York Times there is this group trying to bring a pirate ship to Tampa. They tried that here in Boston, we strongly protested, and ran it away."

Since the ship had more of a historical connection to Boston than to Tampa and the African American community in Boston didn't want it, then a serious red flag was raised and caused me to believe it was my duty to organize a similar resistance in Tampa.

The problem was that this ship, the Whydah Galley was

a 300-ton vessel built in London in 1715, was originally commissioned as a slave ship. Its maiden voyage was to Africa to transport slaves to Jamaica. It was later captured en route home by a pirate named Black Sam Bellamy. Bellamy and crew then headed north to clean the ship, divide the loot, and make plans for its crew members. It is also believed Bellamy was on an "independent frolic" to see a woman in Wellfleet, Massachusetts. However, before they arrived in Wellfleet, the ship was overtaken by a storm and sank off the coast of Cape Cod in 1717.

Bernstein and Betts wanted to construct a seventy million dollar for-profit pirate museum on Tampa's waterfront using the Whydah Galley as a full-scale centerpiece of this entertainment complex. The Whydah Pirate Complex would include a full-scale replica of the ship, an exploration of the Whydah's slave ship history, theatrical re-enactments of pirate hangings, artifacts, and a holographic image of Black Sam Bellamy.

I concluded that this whole idea was an insult that would trivialize slavery through an association with piracy. And to do so for profit was insult compounded. To make this point, I promptly set about to organize in Tampa opposition to this project. Primary among those who joined the resistance were Rev. Arthur Jones, James Ransom, Otis Anthony, Joanna Tokley, and James A. Hammond. We met in my law office for more than a year as we successfully battled the idea of bringing such a project to Tampa.

I argued, the developers showed no evidence of racial sensitivity and the city officials excluded blacks from negotiations. Our protest caught Mayor Sandy Freedman's attention for they were dangling 350 permanent jobs in front of her. A meeting was called to address the issues. Mayor Freedman trusted the complex's developers to treat the racial concerns in a historically accurate fashion. We didn't.

We initially rejected the entire idea. However, after some back and forth, we offered a fair path to a solution. We decided not to prejudge and requested the developers fully present their plans to us. Since we didn't claim to be experts, we offered to further make it fair and judicious by convening a panel of experts to review and report their findings. We would assemble university level experts from wherever they existed in the United States. The experts would render their opinions to us, not to the developers, but to us; and we retained the right to accept or reject their recommendations.

Given the Whydah Pirate Complex was a for-profit-venture, we considered the expenses incurred by this panel of experts to be a cost to be fully borne by the developers.

Experts were picked from the Black History Department at the University of South Florida, as well as black historians and experts from New York, Memphis, Harvard University, and various other places and institutions around the nation to evaluate this proposal. To gauge local opinion, we had meetings in churches and invited the public at large.

With one exception, the expert opinions were in line with our expectations. The exception was of the experts had somehow been unduly influenced by the developers. Incidentally, George W. Bush, the then governor of Texas, was on the team of developers and served on the Silver Screen Management Company Board of Directors.

Clearly, we had our hands full.

Slavery was not a laughing matter and creating a "theme park" atmosphere around it was offensive. I also did not consider freeing slaves and turning them into thieves a redeeming factor. Pirates are thieves.

Several years later, in 2006, the Museum of Science and Industry (MOSI) here in Tampa tried another angle. They attempted to bring the Whydah artifacts to town as a traveling exhibit sponsored by National Geographic. From our perspective, the Whydah was a bad idea in 1991, and it was still a bad idea in 2006.

Throughout, it was our firm belief that African Americans were not looking for a standing reminder of the darkest hour of their existence. Certainly, we were not interested in having a carnival-like sideshow where people pay fifteen dollars a pop to see a ship previously involved in slavery - the most abominable and inhumane act ever committed by humans against other humans in the history of humankind. The idea was abandoned.

Privileged to Meet Some Great Lawyers Along the Way

Growing up in Mulberry didn't offer me an opportunity, as a youngster, to see and know any lawyers. Indeed, I was a college student at FAMU before I came to know any lawyers, black or white. I came to know of the law faculty at the FAMU Law School, and a Pensacola lawyer, Charles F. Wilson, who came to Tallahassee from time to time to defend student civil rights demonstrators and bus boycotters.

As a FAMU freshman, I met Attorney Jewel Stradford Rogers-LaFontant. She traveled from Chicago to Tallahassee to offer her legal services with the criminal prosecution of four white men who, in September of 1961, had forcibly gang raped a FAMU co-ed near the FAMU campus.

While a student at the Howard University Law School, I had the good fortune to meet and learn from some great lawyers and law professors. In my first year, I was taught the law of Real Property by Professor James "Jimmy" Washington, who taught that otherwise boring subject with a passion. It was this good man, in so far as my study of the law and future as a lawyer is concerned, who gave me my break-of-a-lifetime. In that year-long course, with only one examination, he allowed me to retake the exam in his downtown office in Washington D.C., where he served as the Commissioner for Public Conveyances. He even made understandable the legendary puzzle of "The Rule in Shelly's Case." No, I don't know it now.

Likewise, I was taught and mentored by Professor Jeanus Parks, who taught labor law and granted me the opportunity to serve him as a research assistant.

Professor Herbert O. Reed to whom, as president of the National Bar Association, I presented the association's highest award: the C. Francis Stradford Award.

Before and after I graduated, I had the high honor to meet and admire a Philadelphia lawyer named Cecil Moore. In Philadelphia, the question on the street was:

"Who is the best lawyer in Philadelphia?" The response was: "Cecil Moore - when he is drunk." It was then asked, "Who is the second best lawyer in Philadelphia?" The response was: "Cecil Moore - when he is sober."

I had the occasion to meet Mr. Moore while I was still in law school when he was invited to speak to my class. He was not the normal silk stockings type of lawyer. However, the school officials were smart enough to expose us to him in about 1965.

Some years later, about 7:00 a.m., at a National Bar Association breakfast meeting in New York in 1972 at the Waldorf Astoria Hotel, my table-mate was Cecil Moore. The breakfast began with a half of a grapefruit. Even though it was 7:00 a.m., Mr. Moore pulled out a pint of Bourbon whiskey from his inside coat pocket and poured about a quarter of it into his grapefruit. He then took his spoon and fully consumed it before the entre arrived. In my book, he was no less great.

For several years, Leon Sullivan, a preacher and at one time a member of the Board of Directors of General Motors, sponsored an activity in Africa known as the "African/African American Summit."

On one occasion, we traveled to Pretoria, the capital city of the nation of South Africa. There, we were received at the State House by President Nelson Mandela. I actually embraced him when we met and told him how proud I was to be a fellow lawyer.

I had a camera attached to the belt on my waist; I was not supposed to have it. Security had not detected it, nor had I given it any thought. I didn't realize I still had the camera until the "Mandela Kodak moment" happened. I wanted a photograph, but with security and their high-powered weapons guarding Mandela, I dared not reveal that I had this illegal camera still in my possession. I was scared to death and missed the moment. Over my life as a lawyer, I accumulated a lot of photographs of a lot of people, regretfully, I didn't get one with Mandela – even though the opportunity was there.

While I was genuinely fascinated with Mandela, I was also awed by the rise to power orchestrated by Robert Mugabe in the nation then known as Rhodesia – now Zimbabwe. My admiration for this vertically challenged lawyer was not diminished, even though he later became persona non-grata in some places, including the United States. Some thought he held office too long.

Considering that F. W. de Klerk voluntarily relinquished power as president of the Nation of South Africa (under apartheid), the world knows that his decision was due to a series of factors, including world opinion, pressure, boycotts, and being financially squeezed. So, de Klerk simply turned the country over to the black majority. At the same time, Mandela was released from prison on Robben Island after twenty seven years. Mandela essentially walked out of prison and into the presidency. Yes, they had an election, but the prison release and the voluntary transfer of power was very much arranged.

When Mandela assumed the presidency, white people were left in control of everything economically important, except governmental offices. However, in some sense, they were still in control of the government. The South Africans under Mandela were "given" their freedom, they did not "take" their freedom. In Mulberry, it is believed that the power to give includes the power to take away.

In stark contrast Robert Mugabe, a lawyer in the Nation of Rhodesia, went to war against Prime Minster Ian Smith, a white British renegade, who wound up controlling Rhodesia. Mugabe rebelled, he was captured and imprisoned for nearly twelve years before he escaped into the bush. There, he put together an army and returned to wage a successful war against Ian Smith. Mugabe and his army "took" their freedom. In the world genuine freedom, it is better to "take" than to "receive".

In my presence, at a state dinner of about five-hundred people, Mugabe shared with those present the offer he had made as he prepared to take control of the newly-named Nation of Zimbabwe: "For all the whites who are here, you are welcome to stay. But if the sight of blacks in control of their nation and its government gives you a problem – then you need to leave now."

Many whites did stay, including Ian Smith. Mugabe went on to say, "Ian Smith is alive and living right here in Zimbabwe, and for so long as he behaves himself, he will be fine. But if he tries to repeat his previous conduct, I will kill him." I heard those words by Mugabe with my own ears.

A few years later, some of Mugabe's countrymen came to him and said, "Mr. President, I thought we won the war." Mugabe assured them they had. They challenged: "Well if we won the war, why is it that whites still control ninety eight percent of the farm land?" Mugabe assured them he would take some action regarding the matter. However, when he didn't move on the matter as fast as they thought, they began setting fires to white-owned farms.

White farmers collaborated and requested that Mugabe do something to stop the destruction. They argued that the land was theirs and that it had been in their families for years and years.

Mugabe responded saying, "Stop right there. You keep telling me about your land. Let me tell you something: when you show me my land in Europe, I will show you your land here."

Robert Mugabe was a "baaad" brother who, in my view, should be more highly regarded.

Another lawyer I met after I was admitted to The Bar in 1967, was Dudley Thompson. I met him at a Florida Chapter, National Bar Association meeting held in Kingston, Jamaica. Thompson was one of the speakers. His title was "Minister of State in the office of the Prime Minister."

Before I turn from the Mother Land, I desire to share with you the name and translation of the fallen, now deceased, leader of what was formerly known as Zaire. He was not a lawyer and I never actually met him in person - although I did see him from a distance during a Bastille Day Parade in downtown Paris. His name, but even more so the translation of his name sufficiently impressed me.

His Name: MOBUTU SESE SEKO KUKU NEGBENDU WAZA BANGA

Translation: "The all-powerful warrior who, because of his endurance and inflexible will to win, will go from conquest to conquest leaving fire in his wake!"

It was not Thompson's political office that impressed us so much as it was his standing as a lawyer. He was a member of the Queen's Council (QC) which is the highest office a lawyer can hold in the British Empire. Which meant he could practice law anywhere in the Empire and at various times the Empire was almost all over the world. Thus the adage, "The sun never sets on the Union Jack," referring to the British flag.

One of Thompson's most famous international trials involved his successful defense of Jomo Kenyatta in what was known as the Mau Mau trials in the African nation of Kenya.

In addition to those mentioned thus far, there are several men in the legal profession, worthy of mention, who influenced my career as a lawyer. Some of them opened doors for me and others stood with or supported me as I opened the doors myself. All of them, by example, guided me in my effort to be a good lawyer. A partial listing of those lawyers include: James W. Cobb, Thomas James "T.J." Cunningham, Fred D Gray, Donald Lee Hollowell, John Arthur Jones, James Kynes, Jeanus Parks, Matthew Perry, Herbert O. Reid, Francisco Rodriguez, David Shear, Chesterfield Smith, William Reese Smith, Jr., Orzo Thaddeus "OT" Wells, Edward Frank Bell, Lorenzo Williams, and Charles Wilson.

Black Judges Matter

A court in Florida, and in much of the South, the presence of black judges did not begin in earnest until the 1970s. In 1972, Governor Reubin Askew appointed Thomas J. Reddick of Fort Lauderdale as Florida's. Judge Reddick proved to be fair on the issue of race to all who appeared before him.

In 1974, I was a judicial candidate for the County Court of Tampa, Hillsborough County, Florida. I came close but lost to my white opponent. Of course, had I been elected, I too would have been fair on issue of race to all who would have appeared before me.

Speaking of judicial fairness, on the issue of race, I would be remiss if I neglected to reveal that I spent some portion of every day of my half-century practice of law worrying and hoping that the judges hearing my cases would be fair, on the issue of race, to me – and to my clients.

It is a fact that 99.7% of the judges before whom I appeared were white, and at the same time, 99.7% of the lawyers who were my opponents were also white. Therefore, almost on a daily basis, I had to somehow convince myself that I would receive fair and impartial treatment by white judges as compared to my white lawyer opponents.

With the advent of the black judge, a rather interesting and slightly amusing phenomenon occurred. White lawyers appearing against me before black judges were concerned whether they would be treated fairly. Not to worry, nearly all black judges were fair and impartial to a fault.

Unfortunately, there were a few black judges who went overboard to make white lawyers comfortable when opposed by black lawyers.

Finally, we had some black judges who would avoid public interaction or conversation with black lawyers. They feared that some passersby would get the wrong impression of their commitment to fairness and impartiality. In fact, they would virtually run from black lawyers to avoid being seen with them in the hallways of the courthouse. Fortunately, there were only a few judges in this category.

♪ *"Believe I'll run on*
see what the end is gonna be" ♪

Chapter 8

The Quest for Public Office

"Real presence, even without the power of a political office, can bring about meaningful change." WHD

"Dawson has blended a law practice with a dedicated lifelong pursuit of racial equality and justice. The son of a phosphate worker from Mulberry, he worked his way through college, served as an officer in the Army and arrived in Tampa in 1966 to become the first black assistant city attorney. In the Years since then, he has pushed ceaselessly for electoral reforms to give minorities a chance at public office."

The most elusive thing in my adult life was my unsuccessful efforts to gain elective public office. I spent a substantial part of my professional years advocating and litigating the rights of blacks to have meaningful representation in their state and local governments. While my efforts did meet with some success, I personally was never able to pass through the doors that opened due to my efforts.

> ♪ *"The Lord is blessing me right now oh right now, he woke me up this morning and started me on my way"* ♪

I personally made five hard-fought attempts for a seat in the Florida House of Representatives (HOR), one campaign for County Judge (JUD) and one for the Florida State Senate (FSS). They are listed here:

```
1970 HOR  – lost in run off to Julian Lane
1972 JUD  – lost to Tom Miller
1974 HOR  – lost in run off to Ray C. Knopke
1982 HOR  – lost in run off to James Hargrett
1992 FSS  – lost in run off to James Hargrett
2006 HOR  – lost to Betty Reed
2008 HOR  – lost to Betty Reed
```

I believe I hold the record for being a candidate in more party run-off elections for the Florida Legislature than anyone else in Florida history, ultimately to have never served in the legislature. If I am correct, then that record may never be broken because Florida later eliminated party run-off elections. Clearly, the Lord had other plans.

When I first arrived in Tampa, in June of 1966, I made my presence known as the first and only black person working in the Federal Courthouse. I was a law clerk/attorney with the NLRB. In my spare time, I acquainted myself with the state and local electoral systems and the people manipulating them.

As an avid newspaper reader, I discovered that in Hillsborough County there was an at-large multi-member delegation of eight (8) state representatives representing Hillsborough County in the Florida House of Representatives. I also recognized that there was a master plan to add Pasco, Citrus and Hernando Counties to the Hillsborough County Multi-Member District. Three additional seats, for a total of eleven (11) representatives. The idea was to give the additional three counties a representative in the House.

This new four-county multi-member district stretched from near the Suwannee River Bridge in Citrus County to the Manatee County Line – some 100 miles or more, north to south. The then editor of the Tampa Tribune daily newspaper, James Clendenen, who had his thumb on the area. He used his paper to urge candidates and voters from Hillsborough to refrain from voting for Hillsborough candidates and gobbling up the three new seats. In his mind, and in the minds of those persons in Tallahassee who hatched this plan, those seats were intended to provide representation for Pasco, Citrus and Hernando counties – because in their minds counties deserved representation, regardless of how small in population.

Well, I remembered that in 1962 the Supreme Court of the United States decided a case by the name of Baker vs. Carr, 269 U.S. 186. That decision stood for the proposition that representation is premised on the notion of one man, one vote. Stated otherwise, people, not governmental entities, were entitled to be represented. At the time, there were more black people in Hillsborough County than the total number of people in the other three counties combined. At the very same time, black people in Hillsborough County had no representation in the Florida House of Representatives - nor the Florida Senate for that matter. In my mind, it was patently unfair and legally inappropriate to expand the multi-member Hillsborough District and thereby dilute and deny representation for black people of Hillsborough County.

So, I called a meeting and asked a group of black fathers of Hillsborough County to come together to discuss this unfair political plan because it would further minimize the voting rights of the black people in Hillsborough. While C. Blythe Andrews, Sr. was only one of those black fathers who knew me, several of them did come to the meeting.

At that meeting, we formed a coalition, met with some members of the legislative delegation and made known our objections to this plan that ignored us and favored the adjacent counties. While we failed, at that time, to effect the desired changes, we tried and it was the beginning of changes that would occur in later years.

1970 FL House of Representatives

Since we could not beat them, in 1970, I decided to make the effort to join them. I ran for an at-large seat in the Florida House of Representatives, District 64. All of my opponents were white, and included: Angelo Frank Favata, Pat Frank, Gilbert Hyde, Julian B. Lane, Steve Ross, Mike Scionti and W. D. (Doug) West, Sr. Chief among my opponents, were Julian B. Lane, the then immediate past mayor of the City of Tampa; Pat Frank, an early female politician, who later held political offices for a number of years; and Mike Scionti, who later became the local Democratic Party chairman.

In 1970, we still had multi-member districts and that meant, if I wanted to represent the good people of Belmont Heights, Progress Village, East and West Tampa in the Florida House of Representatives, I had to stand election by people in Temple Terrace, Plant City, Dade City, New Port Richey, Springhill, Brooksville, Crystal River, Homosassa, and Inverness.

While I was young, able and ready to represent the people of that sprawling district in Tallahassee, t'was not to be. I lost to Julian Lane in a run-off election.

1972 Hillsborough County Judgeship

In 1972, I ran for Hillsborough County Judge. Again, my opponent, Thomas A. Miller Sr., was white. Miller won. Had I won, I would have been the first black elected official in Hillsborough County, Florida since 1888 when Cyrus Charles, Henry Brumick, and Joseph Walker were the three black persons elected to the Tampa City Council, in that order, in the mid-1800s. Charles also served as a Hillsborough County Commissioner from 1868 to 1871.

As I see it, my campaign was unsuccessful only in that it was not won. It was, nevertheless, a moral victory when viewed in the context of the politics of Hillsborough County, Florida, at the time.

It was the best near miss of any black candidate in Hillsborough County to that date. I was the first black candidate to receive in excess of forty percent of the votes cast: 19,937 for me and 25,538 for Miller.

Among the positive lessons learned from that campaign was that an increasing number of white people were willing to vote for a black candidate. Regrettably, a negative lesson learned was there were black hustlers who openly campaigned against black candidates. To them, the white man's ice was colder than the black man's ice.

The reason I was willing to climb that uphill battle was because, at the time, whites held all elected positions. They controlled business, land, utilities and most of the other critical aspects of life. Of course, all of these matters were directly affected by politics. I told the then Tampa Times newspaper: "My defeat left blacks with non-existent representation. We were a community in exile."

At the same time, the election of James Sanderlin, a black St. Petersburg lawyer, as a judge of the Pinellas County Court, begged the question: "What made Hillsborough County so different?"

An article titled "Good Guys Win & Good Guys Lose in Area Politics" commented regarding my campaign in the following manner:

> *"It is rare indeed to find someone who is a 'Natural' politician. ...Warren Dawson definitely had the "The Look of a Leader." More importantly, it doesn't stop there that's only the beginning. Intellectually, he's a giant. His mind functions with a clear, crisp quickness of a complicated computer. Right on time and right on target. Many of his colleagues agreed, Warren would have carried to the Judgeship, had he won, the same high degree of polish and expertise that is evident in his successful law practice. He ran a good campaign, a clean campaign. He threw mud at none and proudly ran on his record. And he ran well. It was a close race. His opponent did not get a landslide victory. Anything but. Only a few, paltry votes, less than five thousand, separated the two contestants. It was gratifying to note that thousands of white voters supported Warren's candidacy, giving positive testimony to the confidence his great ability fosters."*

Less than two years after my candidacy for a Hillsborough County Judgeship, a county judgeship vacancy occurred. I promptly made application to the Governor requesting that he fill that vacancy by appointing me. At the time, I thought my chances of appointment were pretty good, given my recent broad citizen support for the position.

Fortunately (for the black citizens of the county), the Governor was moved to make a historical decision by appointing the first black judge in Hillsborough County, i.e., George E. Edgecomb. George was my schoolmate at the Howard University School of Law. He graduated in the class of 1967. I graduated in the class of 1966.

It was a fact that George was a good man, a good lawyer and he deserved the appointment. But then, so did

I. Being a Hillsborough County native was in George's favor and he had not irritated any white people by running against them, as I had done.

Judge Edgecomb served as a Hillsborough County Judge for only 2-3 years before his untimely death in 1976. The history surrounding his appointment drove the decision to name the Hillsborough County Court House in his honor. The black bar association was also named for him and his wife benefited by getting elected to the Hillsborough County School Board.

I submit that the chain of events that directly led to this judicial history began when I made the bold decision in 1972, as a black lawyer, to run for the position of County Judge. Among other things, that decision sent a clear message that black people both desired and deserved representation in the local judiciary and that there were capable black lawyers available to serve.

1974 FL House of Representatives, Group 67

In 1974, once again I sought election to the Florida House of Representatives in the sprawling geographical area of Hillsborough, Pasco, Citrus, and Hernando counties. As before, I was the only black candidate in the race. My opponents were: Julian N. Graham, Angelo L. Greco, and Ray C. Knopke. Knopke had previously served in the Florida Senate. I lost to Knopke in a runoff election.

Reapportionment -1980

It was Morris Milton, a black lawyer from St. Petersburg, Florida, who was then serving as the lawyer for the NAACP State Conference of Branches, and I who worked together to eliminate this so-called multi-member district system. Under that system, only one black person had succeeded in getting elected to the Florida House of Representatives. His name was Joe Lang Kershaw, a former high school football coach in Miami. Kershaw was followed by Gwendolyn Cherry, a Miami lawyer.

Milton and I, along with other fair-minded Floridians, owe a great amount of thanks to then State Representative, Lee Moffitt, the person for whom the Tampa based Moffitt Cancer Center is named. Moffitt, as chairman of the House Reapportionment Committee, led the decision on how the House would elect its members. While he could have stuck with the existing multi-member districts – he chose instead, to heed our demand for single-member districts.

As mentioned earlier, the biggest opposition to single-member districts came from none other than James Clendenen, the then editor, and publisher of the Tampa Tribune Newspaper. He had a scolding dislike for what he called "ward-politics". Despite Clendenen, and his well-known position, Moffitt summoned the strength to do the right thing albeit against the grain of the powerful publisher of the dominant daily newspaper in his hometown.

At the time, the chairman of the Senate Reapportionment Committee was none other than Dempsey Barron, who had served in the Florida Senate for many years. Some said he was "The Man" in the Florida Senate. Moffitt's early decision regarding the House tipped the momentum in favor of single-member districts. Barron ultimately followed Moffitt's lead and agreed to install single-member districts in the Florida Senate.

This change in both the Florida Senate and the Florida House of Representatives presented, for the first time, a meaningful opportunity for blacks to elect persons of their choice to both chambers. In the years that followed, the black citizens of Florida, under the system of single-member districts, have experienced some success in electing persons of their choice to the Florida Legislature.

1982 FL House of Representatives, District 63

In 1982, I was a candidate for the Florida House of Representatives, in District 63. This district was newly created and consciously structured to give blacks an opportunity to elect a representative of their choice.

In past attempts for elective public office, I ran for positions where the electorate was overwhelmingly white and against white opponents. This time, all my opponents were black. They included: George Washington Butler, Leslie Miller, and James Hargrett. Of course, it was my advocacy, along with that of Morris Milton, a black St. Petersburg lawyer, that was the primary force that pushed the adoption of single-member districts in the Florida Legislature.

That blacks in this new district then had a meaningful opportunity to be elected, was not wasted on those who may have previously desired to be a candidate for public office. Rather than facing the uphill battle of running against a white opponent in an election with an overwhelmingly white electorate, they had simply deferred their dreams until a more realistic opportunity was in place.

By example, Hargrett who had been my campaign treasurer in a previous election effort against white opponents, was now moved to become a candidate himself – against me. The boys in Mulberry remind us that the bird who brings the worm to the nest has no guarantee to dine.

It was Hargrett and I in the runoff. He ultimately won this new House seat made possible, in part, by my relentless advocacy. The Legislature had realigned and created a single-member district which had a competitive number of black people. However, blacks did not dominate. The population might have been 52% black, but the registered voter population might have been closer to 40%. Symbolically however, this was a black seat – actually, a plausible white candidate could have won it. In point of fact, the white electorate could and did, at Hargrett's behest, significantly affect the outcome.

It was in that context that Hargrett in the runoff election against me began to articulate that I was a race troublemaker. Because I had been involved in all kinds of civil rights activities, including school desegregation, he painted me as someone to fear as a creator of hate between the races. That was his pitch to white people. Along the way, I believe if some political scientist truly analyzed the voting in this instance, they would surely find I carried the black, but not white, vote. In a real sense, I was unjustly treated for the justice I had demanded.

Warren vs. Tampa 1980-1988

On May 26, 1980, a lawsuit was filed by Willie Warren and Carl Warren against the City of Tampa and Hillsborough County challenging the at-large procedure by which members of the City Council and the Board of County Commissioners were elected (hereinafter "Warren I"). The Plaintiffs alleged in Warren I that the City and the County at-large election systems violated the First, Fourteenth and Fifteenth Amendments to the Constitution of the United States, Sec. 2 of the Voting Rights Act, and 42 U.S.C. Sec. 1983.

The Court conducted a fairness hearing on March 28, 1988. Thereafter, the parties submitted demographic data, and affidavits from their respective expert witnesses, supporting their contention that the four single-member districts, three members-at-large system of voting now utilized in the City of Tampa was a fair and reasonable system. Plaintiffs filed the depositions of Mr. Al Davis and Mr. Carl Warren. Both parties filed their post-fairness hearing memorandum on June 23, 1988.

Ultimately, the court approved the settlement agreement whereby both the City of Tampa and the County of Hillsborough would elect their city council and county commission members, respectively, utilizing a system of four representatives elected from districts and three at-large. The Court's approval of this new system was over the strenuous objection of two members of the Class - both black lawyers (Warren Hope Dawson and Ricky Williams) - who took the position that counsel of record for the Class should have, but had not, pressed for all representatives to be elected from districts.

1992 FL State Senate, District 21

In 1992, I was a candidate for the Florida State Senate, in District 21. That district was newly created and consciously structured to give blacks in Tampa Bay Area (including portions of Hillsborough, Pinellas, Manatee and Polk Counties) an opportunity to elect a Senator of their choice. My opponents were James Hargrett and Rudolph Bradley. Both black.

Hargrett, as an existing member of the House, had significant input into the creation and the footprint of this new Senate District. In this regard, it was more than a mere coincidence that the district boundaries managed to exclude my residence and the residence of Sadie Martin, the then mayor of Plant City. Both Ms. Martin and I were potential Hargrett opponents for this new seat in the Florida Senate. Martin did not run, and I changed my residence so that I could run.

In the August 24, 1992, issue of the Tampa Tribune, the endorsement of my candidacy was a comprehensive documentation of my knowledge, experience, accomplishments and confirmation that I possessed the necessaries to become an effective legislator in the Florida Senate. The newspaper editorial said as follows:

"... Dawson has blended a law practice with a dedicated lifelong pursuit of racial equality and justice. The son of a phosphate worker from Mulberry, he worked his way through college, served as an officer in the Army and arrived in Tampa in 1966 to become the first black assistant city attorney. In the years since then, he has pushed ceaselessly for electoral reforms to give minorities a chance at public office. He was a strong advocate for city Council districts for single-member legislative districts, and he represents the National Association for the Advancement of Colored People

in the desegregation case of Hillsborough County school system. Dawson has served as an attorney for the Hillsborough County legislative delegation and has been on the County Civil Service Board a charter review commission and the board of Florida Rural Legal Services for the poor and the Hillsborough County Criminal Justice Planning Committee. He achieved a particular distinction in 1982 when he was elected president of the National Bar Association, an organization of black attorneys. And then there is the Mystic Crew of Gasparilla, Dawson more than anyone else engineered the public debate over racial exclusion on the part of the city's premier private social club using the 1990 Super Bowl as a public relations hammer. He led the coalition of African-American organizations to demand that the all-white crew integrate to avoid embarrassment to the city at a time when national attention was about to be focused on it. A year later the crew admitted four black members and the Gasparilla is stronger and more open than ever. Dawson took on some powerful people and institutions when he did that. It was a daring act, and painful though it was for everyone involved, the community is better for it. Dawson demonstrated backbone tenacity, diplomacy, and courage in his handling of that task. All attributes that could make for a formidable State Senator to represent the voters of the sprawling far-flung District 21. Dawson deserves their vote on September 1."

The primary results were: Hargrett 44 percent; Dawson, 34 percent, and Bradley 21 percent. With no single candidate having more than 50 percent, Hargrett and I advanced to a runoff. Bradley was eliminated. Hargrett clearly won the runoff in October with 9,791(62%) of the votes to my 6,090 (38%).

In the perfect world of what might-have-been, should-have-been, or could-have-been: it later occurred to me that when Hargrett vacated the House seat he had won by defeating me in 1982, I should have run again for that seat in the House. Of course, it is also appropriate to remember that in many instances even hindsight is not 20/20.

2006 FL House of Representatives, District 59

In 2006, again I was a candidate for the Florida House of Representatives, in District 59. My opponents were Betty Reed and Hakim Aquil.

> ♪ *"Lord, I'm running trying to make a 100 cause 99 1/2 just won't do"* ♪

A 2001 Florida Election Reform eliminated second primary elections: known as party run-off elections. Run-offs were conducted when three (3) or more candidates of the same party sought election, but no one of them succeeded in getting 51% or more of the votes cast.

Hakim pitched himself as Hakim "The Dream" Aquil. Betty Reed was declared the winner with less than 51% of the votes. The breakdown was Reed 47.47%; Dawson 43.65%; and Hakim 8.88%. As indicated, party run-off elections had previously been eliminated.

Aside from losing by less than 300 votes, the most memorable and unfortunate occurrence happened on one Saturday afternoon in June of 2006. I was campaigning door-to-door on a fire-cracker hot day and decided to go to my law office and get a cold drink of water.

When I arrived at my office complex, Management had allowed a film crew to paint a temporary mural on the building's outside wall. There were people everywhere.

Every parking space was filled, and there were tables on the sidewalk blocking the entrance to the front door of my office. Basically, using it as a staging area and I couldn't get into my office.

I asked a member of the crew to adjust such that I could enter my law office. Reluctantly, he complied. But after I entered my office to get that drink of water, the member complained about my presence to the two-person police detail hired as their security.

The next thing I realized was a policeman had actually entered my office and confronted me with the question; "What is your problem?" It seemed to me like a very good question being asked of the very wrong person by the very wrong person. After I asked the policemen to please step out of my office, the situation escalated. I was manhandled, battered, and handcuffed by the one officer who seemed overly aggressive and with a combative temperament (not dissimilar to that captured on film of police mistreatment of black men). At 6-feet 4-inches and with my arms handcuffed behind my back, I was stuffed into the back of a broiling hot police cruiser that had been sitting in the sun for most of the day. Later, a sergeant arrived, we talked, and he gave the order to release me.

The officer with the bad temperament then took great and unnecessary pain to write in his citation that I was a candidate for the legislature. The assistant Tampa Park manager later apologized and confirmed that the crew had permission to film the mural but not to interfere with tenant's ability to conduct their commercial business.

A Black Male - No Exception

2008 FL House of Representatives, District 59

In 2008, I was a candidate for the Florida House of Representatives, in District 59. My opponent was Betty Reed, the incumbent. With a track record of her performance as solid evidence, I waged an aggressive campaign. I maintained that Obama was the change the nation needed and Dawson was the change District 59 needed.

As for Representative Reed, I felt it my duty to inform the electorate of her lackluster record in the Legislature. In that regard, I created a flyer with the shameful details.

However, to her credit, Representative Reed successfully ran an "underdog" – "grass roots" campaign, the kind of campaign that black people strongly relate to. Once again I was reminded that in politics in general, and particularly in the black community, "I like" trumps "IQ" most of the time.

Political Reflections

Politics taught me a lot about life and people. Having devoted many years and resources to the effort of gaining elected public office, the lessons learned have guided my decisions in other matters.

For example, I learned that if you experience some calamity, such as the death of a close family member; your house burns down, or you fail to get a promotion and lose your job altogether, those are not the occasions when you find out who are your real friends. In such circumstances, your distant friends and even some of your avowed critics will show you some compassion or lend you a hand. But, if you really want to find out who are your real friends – then my friend, run for public office.

Politics is a lot about time and place. Both need to be right. In the early years, I ran for office knowing that my chances for success were not good. Beginning in 1970, I was, however, thoroughly convinced that it was important to make the statement that black people desired, deserved and were qualified to hold elective office in state and local government.

♪ *"Through it all*
I learned to trust in God
I learned to depend on his word" ♪

So, against the odds, I ran against white candidates in situations where winning was remote at best. It could be said that in the 1970s I was ahead of the times – or too young, too fresh and yes, too black. Realizing that more was expected of me – maybe more than I had to give – I just kept saying to myself:

Despite my courageous efforts, it became clear that the playing field was tilted against a black person getting elected to the Florida Legislature. Campaigning in multi-member districts was brutal. So, to change and level the playing field, something had to change.

I submit that my willingness to engage in those battles had a significant influence in bringing about single-member districts, which is now taken for granted by many people who hold office. The history of the creation of single-member districts was an ugly fight, and it was out in the open for the entire world to see.

Early on, there were only a few blacks willing to face and confront this "institutional wrong." A wrong that denied blacks full and equal access to the political process. The courage to go eyeball-to-eyeball when seemingly "hope unborn had died," was clearly required to correct this injustice.

In the 1980's, when we finally established single-member districts in the legislature, in the county and city offices as well, it could be said that I was no longer young, not fresh and not popular. Thus, my fate as a candidate was decided by the "I like" trumps "I Q" phenomenon.

Although it is more than probable that I will not ever personally hold an elected public office, I am nevertheless left with the eternal satisfaction that my advocacy contributed greatly in leveling the playing field so that others could serve. In that regard, I am reminded of the words of Martin Luther King, Jr., "I may not get there with you, but one day we'll get to the Promised Land."

Chapter 9

There is Always a Way

"What do you do until the revolution comes? Make things happen!" "Real presence, even without the power of the elected office, can bring about meaningful change" WHD

President Jimmy Carter, Warren Hope Dawson

President Ronald Regan, Warren Hope Dawson

Having a seat at the table when critical issues are being discussed, and historical decisions are being made, can be more powerful than titles. I made sure I was at the right tables and that the voice of black people was heard.

So, what do you do until the revolution comes? Make things happen because there is always a way to get a job done. As highlighted in the chapter on my competitive nature, before, during, and after running for political office, I always tried to position myself to make a difference.

Frequently, I functioned as a minister plenipotentiary without portfolio. Although I knew the issues and was full of ideas about how to address them, I was without position or authority to make the needed decisions. Yet, I was determined to push for what I believed to be the position of the black community.

Elected or not, I saw myself as the community's ambassador. This was particularly true during the time frames when the community had little or no elected representation.

A few examples of where I was among the ranks of those making far-reaching decisions include: Meeting with President Carter in the White House; Serving as a member of the Hillsborough Charter Commission; the Delegation Attorney for the 1976 Hillsborough County Legislative Delegation; Serving on the Rules Committee of the Democratic National Convention; As the Labor Attorney for the National Labor Relations Board; Chairman, Tampa Unified Construction Trades Board; Chairman, Hillsborough County Civil Service Board; and the Judicial Council of the African Methodist Episcopal

Vice President George W Bush, Warren Hope Dawson

Church. I was also an active member of the Florida Probation & Parole Qualifications Committee, the Tampa Urban League Board, the Tampa Red Cross Board, the Advisory Board of the Tampa Bay Buccaneers, the U.S. Department of Justice National Advisory Board, District Board of Trustees for Hillsborough Community College (HCC), Board of Directors of WMNF Radio (Non-commercial FM community radio station), my beloved Alpha Phi Alpha Fraternity and was the Hillsborough Legislative Delegation Attorney.

Hillsborough County Civil Service Board

Seated from left to right- William R. McCelland; Warren Hope Dawson, Chairman and Diana Almeida Standing from left to right- Victor Vizcaino; Dennis Diecidue and Thomas Stringer

At a point in time when all employees of the County were subject to the Civil Service Board that was designed to act as a single portal for screening and hiring employees at nearly two dozen county agencies. It also heard workplace grievances, giving County employees extra protection beyond due process rights under the law. Its well-intended mission as an independent agency was to keep county employment free of cronyism and political patronage. I followed C. Blythe Andrews, Sr., as only its second black member. I was later joined by Thomas Stringer, who assisted me in becoming Chairman.

Hillsborough Charter Commission

When an opponent says, "I'll check the City Charter", that document can either shut you down or liberate you to act. When you assist in writing the rules, you have a better chance that they would support your cause.

In 1966, during one of the required public hearing for a charter review of a planned city and county merger, opposition from the black community was strong. I had read every line of the Charter and was displeased with the sections dealing with county-wide voting in the legislative branch and civil service system.

I clearly stated, I viewed the civil service section of the Charter as inappropriate and a perpetuation of the same "mess" we already had. It didn't have an anti-discrimination clause, which meant the department heads would be perpetually in office and continue to block blacks from getting employed. The black community viewed the merger as another maneuver to control government. Among those also voicing their opinions were Dr. William Andrews, Mrs. Mary Alice Dorsett, Mrs. Sylvia Grinan, Mr. James A. Hammond, and Mr. Jerry N. Harvey.

Legislative Delegation Attorney

In 1972, I was hired by the Legislation Delegation from Hillsborough County to be their lawyer during the legislative session for that year. The Delegation consisted of eight State Representatives and three State Senators. While there were admittedly some political reasons for this employment, there also was expressed trust in my legal acumen to do the job - and I did it well.

Bureau of Justice Statistics Advisory Board

During the administration of President Jimmy Carter, I was named as a member of the Bureau of Justice Statistics (BJS), a component of the Office of Justice Programs in the U.S. Department of Justice. The Bureau was first established in December of 1979, and its mission was to collect, analyze, publish, and disseminate information on crime, criminal offenders, victims of crime, and the operation of justice systems at all levels of government.

That data is critical to federal, state, and local policymakers in combating crime and ensuring justice are both efficient and evenhanded. I saw it as my mission on this Board to ensure that crime statistics interpreted by the Justice Department reflect proper and reasoned interpretation. I did not want to have a study on crime utilized to create hysteria for people in general.

This Advisory Board had 21 members. I was the only representative from Florida and one of only four minorities. Among my fellow members were the Attorney General of the State of Kansas and the District Attorney of Los Angeles County California.

Tampa Bay Buccaneer's Advisory Board

Through my Mulberry/Wauchula connection with the McEwen brothers (Red McEwen, a prominent Tampa lawyer and personal friend of Hugh Culverhouse, a Jacksonville tax lawyer who became the first owner of the Tampa Bay Buccaneers and Tom McEwen, the sports editor for the Tampa Tribune Newspaper), I was asked to serve on the NFL Tampa Buccaneers' Advisory Board of Directors.

Even though he was from Jacksonville, Culverhouse was wise enough to select a locally based "board of directors." This board included: Stuart Bryan, whose family owned the Tampa Tribune newspaper; Paul Lake, who headed the St. Petersburg Times newspaper; George Gage, from General Telephone & Electric (GTE) Telephone Company; and Hugh Culbreath, from Tampa Electric (TECO) with George Gage, H.L. Culbreath, Art Pepin, James "Jimmy" Kynes, Sam Davis, James M. "Red"

McEwen, Bob Lowrey, Scott Linder, Lloyd Phillips, Ron Hicks, Dick Pope and myself.

Honorary Doctorate FAMU

On August 5, 2011, in part for my advocacy that brought about a major change in how the Florida legislature, both the Senate and the House, elected its Members on the basis of single-member rather than multi-member districts. This change, in the early 1980s, created meaningful opportunities for Blacks, particularly those who resided in the urban centers of Florida, to elect representatives of their choosing in both the Florida Senate and the Florida House of Representatives.

The decision, on the part of the trustees, the president, the administration, the faculty and the alumni, to honor me with this significant award may have gone unnoticed but for the special attention of the president, Dr. James Ammons and attorney Daryl D. Parks, a then leader on the FAMU Board of Trustees.

FAMU Professor of Military Science, Warren Hope Dawson, President James H. Ammons, and FAMU Professor of Military Science following Honorary Docorate Awards Ceremony

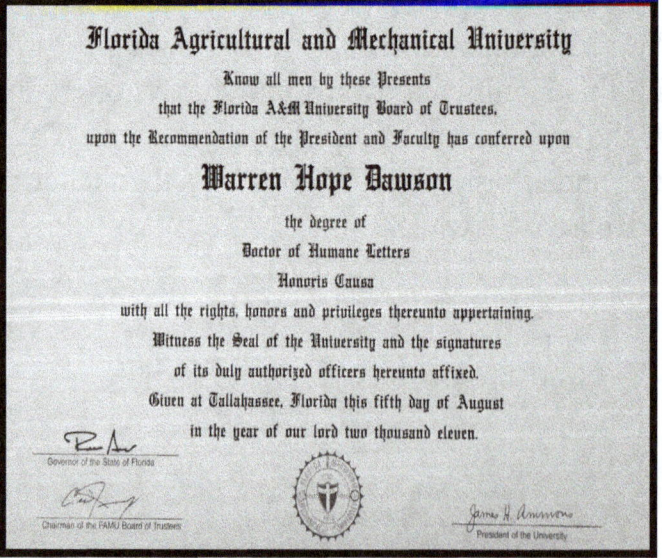

Once In A Lifetime

An ideal bucket list opportunity occurred without warning while on a trip to Rio de Janeiro, Brazil. I stayed at the French hotel, Le Meridian Hotel, on the Copa Cabana Beach.

One morning while on the hotel elevator, several people got on wearing New England Conservatory Orchestra t-shirts. I inquired about the nature of their Brazilian visit and was told they were from Boston and were touring Brazil, sponsored by the Fleet Banks in Boston, which also existed in Brazil.

Their orchestra was performing in a band shell on the beach and they invited me to come. I said, "Sure. But, only if I can conduct." They laughed. I did not. Seeing them around the hotel later during the week, each time I reminded them they had promised I could conduct.

Several days later, I found out the orchestra was having a dress rehearsal, so I attended. When they finished, I yelled, "Hey, remember me? I'm the guy you said you would allow to conduct." The conductor then started the orchestra in the very familiar military faithful, Stars and Stripes Forever, and invited me to take the baton. I, of course, knew the tune very well and proceeded to conduct as if my life depended on it.

When finished, the conductor offered one of the t-shirts to me and then informed me that if the opportunity I had just experienced had occurred back in Boston, I would have been expected to make at least a $25,000 donation to the orchestra. To which I replied, with a smile, "Hey, I am just a country boy from Mulberry, Florida and I don't have any money – but thank you so very much for this unique and memorable experience."

I am now able to say, without fear of correction, "I conducted a symphony orchestra on the Copacabana Beach in Rio de Janeiro, Brazil."

Of course, the mention of Rio brings "Carnival" to mind. While my visits to Rio did not include Carnival, my travels have included Carnival in Trinidad, Mardi Gras in New Orleans and Gasparilla in Tampa.

Most people who know me, are well aware that I am a strong believer in education. Some of them may not know that I have high regard for how formal education is enhanced by travel. I know so well because I am well-traveled. I have been all over North America, from Central America, to South America, to Australia, to Europe, to Asia, to the Middle East, to the Far East and to most of the regions of Africa.

I am particularly proud and enhanced by my travel in Africa. After all, I have held myself out to be an informal student of the continent. Don't forget, I am the African Legal Eagle.

Among my travels to Africa I had the high privilege to meet, embrace, and converse with Nelson Mandela at the State House in Pretoria, South Africa, and Robert Mugabe at a State dinner in Harare, Zimbabwe. I walked through the dungeons of the House of Slaves on the Island of Gorrie in the nation of Senegal.

As I digested what had happened to my ancestors in

that place, including their exit through the "Door of No Return," I was greatly disturbed and thoroughly pissed. I observed the court proceedings, in Arusha, Tanzania, of the International Criminal Tribunal for Rwanda. I was amazed by the Pyramids of Giza located near Cairo, Egypt. As I departed Egypt, I confess to filling two small containers: with rocks from the Pyramids; and water from The Nile River. In other African travel, I had brief visits to the nations of Morocco and Gabon.

My extensive travel over much of the world is very high on the list of things that made me happy.

Living on the Hillsborough River, having a boat was a must.

First to Move In

I was the first black person to buy a home in River Grove Estates, Tampa, Florida. The subdivision is nestled among the trees along the Hillsborough River near or adjacent to 40th Street.

My decision to purchase a home, in 1970, on the Hillsborough River presumably influenced several other blacks to do likewise. Namely: C. Blythe Andrews Jr. owner of the Florida Sentinel Bulletin; Bobby Scott of Metropolitan Insurance; Perry Harvey Jr., International Vice President of the Longshoreman's Union; Abraham Brown, pastor of one the largest churches in the city; and others.

A few more black families moved in, classic white fear and flight fully engaged, consistent with expectations the neighborhood evolved into a predominately black community. Contrary to the countless overly publicized examples of neighborhood decline, this black riverfront community continues to be a highly desirable place to live.

Fulfilling My Mother's Dream

July 2016 at Allen Temple A.M.E.

As I conclude this section, I paused and realized that without a deliberate plan to do so, I have fulfilled and surpassed my mother's ultimate dream. The term P K, as in "Preacher's Kid," and the pressure that comes with it, is well known. I, on the other hand, was a M K, as in "Musician's Kid". As such, I was in church every time the doors opened, even more than a PK.

My mother's talents were attached to nearly everything that happened in the church. To give up so much of your life, you must have unshakable respect for preachers, presiding elders, and bishops and she did. She thought they were next to Jesus. Her greatest dream was to have her son become an ordained minister and to rise in the hierarchy of the church clergy.

In July of 2016, Mother must have sung 1st soprano in heaven when I was elected to an eight-year term as a judge o n the Judicial Council of the African Methodist Episcopal (A.M.E.) Church. Her son is now charged with reviewing the decisions of pastors, elders, and even bishops of the A.M.E. Church - worldwide. The A.M.E. Church has a presence in thirty-five countries on five continents.

From L to R: Bishop Julius Harrison McAllister, Judge Warren Hope Dawson, Bishop Adam Jefferson Richardson Jr. & Bishop John Franklin White

Struck by Lightning

In April of 2018, The Tampa Bay Lightning recognized my community advocacy with its Community Hero Award. A half-time video presentation covered my career and the $50,000.00 award to The Warren Hope Dawson Elementary School Foundation, Inc. (my favorite charity) was presented.

But for the input of the Saturday Morning Breakfast Group and James Ransom, this recognition may not have happened.

Women Legal Trailblazers

With this section, I pay special tribute to some of the many remarkable female attorneys who I encountered during my career.

Patricia Dawson (not related) - came to my office within a few weeks after graduating from high school seeking employment. I hired her as an office clerk and encouraged her to enroll at HCC. I tailored her work hours to accommodate her HCC class schedule. When she graduated from HCC, I encouraged her to attend FAMU. With me as a reference, she secured a law-related job at FAMU. After FAMU, she was able to get into FSU Law School. When she finished there, she returned to Tampa and again worked in my office. Later, I submitted a recommendation for her to work with the Office of the State Attorney.

Patricia Roberts Harris - a law professor at Howard University School of Law, taught me torts and constitutional law. Clearly one of the most articulate persons I've heard in my life. I place her in the general category of Martin Luther King, in terms of her oratory skills.

Dovey Roundtree - a trial lawyer in DC who tried serious criminal cases. I first saw her when she spoke at Howard Law School. I later found out she was once general counsel to the A.M.E. Church. We, as law students, were amazed to learn from her speech that she had advance sheets of the Washington, DC court cases brought to her early each morning before she began her daily routine. By the time she was dressed, she had informed herself on the relevant case rulings made the day before. We were amazed by her diligence.

Marjorie Lawson - one of the first black judges in Washington, DC. was a juvenile judge who also spoke at the Howard Law School. I had a classic crush on her. She, however, was also the wife of Belford Lawson, a great DC lawyer and former national president of Alpha Phi Alpha fraternity. Belford, as it turned out, had been a speaker at FAMU during my undergraduate years.

Rosemary Filipovich - my first boss after law school, was one of the first women to hold the position of regional attorney for the NLRB. She was based in Region 12 in Tampa, covering Georgia and Florida. I reported to the NLRB and to Rosemary Filipovich on June 13, 1966.

Elaine Jones - a great civil rights lawyer and Director

of the NAACP Legal Defense and Education Fund Inc. We worked together on the Manning vs. School Board case in Tampa.

Elizabeth A. Kovachevich - a United States District Judge who presided over the final years of the Manning case. She followed Judges Ben Kretzman and William T. Hodges.

Carol Taylor - a smart young lawyer who was among the first wave of black appellate judges in Florida. She sat on the Fourth District Court of Appeal based in Fort Lauderdale.

Marilyn Holyfield - was my special assistant during my tenure as president of the National Bar Association (NBA). Thanks to her grant writing abilities, my 1982 - 1983 NBA administration had more operational funds than any administrations that followed. I expressed my appreciation for her by appointing her to the Board of the Governors of the American Bar Association (ABA).

Constance Baker Motley - Thurgood Marshall's immediate successor as Director of the NAACP Legal Defense and Education Fund Inc., preceding Elaine Jones as director.

Kaydell Wright - a lawyer and a friend with whom I cooperated to offer legal services.

Gabrielle Kirk McDonald - a Howard Law School classmate. First a federal district judge, and later an international judge as a member of the International Criminal Tribunals of Bosnia and Rowanda. A matchless combination of brains and beauty.

Chapter 10

My Support System

Mr. & Mrs. Warren Hope Dawson

Always A Lady

Through it all I had one wife – my only wife, Joan Delores Brown Dawson - of New Bern, North Carolina. We met in Washington, DC while I was a law student at Howard University, and she was a classroom teacher in the public schools of Arlington County, Virginia.

There of course was Joan of Arc and Joan of New Bern. I admired them both.

My Joan was "Once, Twice, Three Times a Lady," - whom I loved.

Joan, Warren Hope, and Wendy Hope Dawson

In the midst of legendary fights for civil rights for the members of my community, came the most precious fight of all – being a father. In August 1976, Wendy Hope Dawson, my daughter, who brought me joy and all of the responsibility that goes along with me being her "Dad".

My Daughter, Wendy, her Husband, Clarence Bostic, & my Grandchildren Ashley & C J

Grand and Great Grands

I am very fortunate to have had 16 women who comprise my Support Team and they are: Joan Brown Dawson; Wendy Dawson Bostic; Katrena Flowers; Naomi Arron; Bernice Otudeko; Celest Hurst; Saundra Gaulman; Crista Dawson; Wanda Brown; Alline Rivers; Nina Danzey; Jessica Danzey; Alexis Danzey; Monica McCoy Purdy; Jessie Glover; and Dorothy Buster.

Chapter 11

In Conclusion

I began by acknowledging that my life was all about: "The Journey of An African Legal Eagle" because life is often defined by the journey – and not by the destination. The truth of this is confirmed by the following profound statement on the subject:

> *"If ever there was a metaphor to illustrate the importance of the journey over the destination, it is life itself. For everyone who departs from birth is destined for death, so the journey IS life. Savour it!"*
>
> *– Michele Jennae*

Straight out of Mulberry, I was destined to find my niche in Tampa. In the early years, I fought the outsiders' "you're not from here" battle. However, with better than sixty years as a resident, Tampa is my home. I have always felt a special kinship to Tampa because as a boy my mom would often bring me to Tampa as she shopped for new music at the Arthur Smith Music Store and visited the offices of the Florida Sentinel and the Tampa Bulletin Newspapers.

I am comfortable with the fact that I did not set out on this journey to simply make a living – I set out to make a difference and in many ways I succeeded. I helped to make Tampa, Hillsborough County, Florida a better place for all people who call it home – and I did so without ever having held an elective public office.

The Journey of an African Legal Eagle

At 75 - still enjoying the journey

As a trial lawyer for more than fifty years, I have heard a lot of courtroom testimony, but for the years before that I heard a lot of church testimony, which often began with these words:

"I wouldn't take nothing for my journey now."

Mother and Two Sons

On some future appointed day, now known only by the Lord, word will go forth that declares:

"The Eagle – Yes, The African Legal Eagle has landed."

That day was __,__,20__.

For those who mourn his absence in the world,
May also rejoice in his presence with the Lord
May the Lord bless you and keep you
May the Lord make his face to shine upon you,
    and be gracious unto you
May the Lord life up his countenance upon you,
    and give you peace.
        Amen

... and to think I did all that

The Journey

1939	October 17 - Born on a hill in Prairie in a laborers' housing quarters owned by International Mineral Chemical Corporation, a phosphate mining company. Prairie was located two or three miles east of Mulberry, FL.
1945	September – Enrolled in the First Grade at JRE Lee School - in Mulberry, FL.
1947	February – Survived a house fire that destroyed the recently built family home in Mulberry.
1948	March – Grieved, at age nine (9), the death of my Father, Japhus Lloyd Dawson. Also in 1948, grieved the death of my Maternal Grandfather, Adam Warren, and the death of my Uncle, L.R. Warren.
1950	June – Experienced culture shock when my Mother, Naomi Warren Dawson, moved from Mulberry, FL and accepted job at a music house in the heart of downtown Baltimore, MD.
1951	June – Rejoiced over my mother's decision to move from Baltimore back to Mulberry.
1954	June – Graduated, Salutatorian, J.R.E. Lee Jr. High School, Mulberry FL.
1957	June – Graduated, Union Academy High School, Bartow, FL.
1957	September – Enrolled at Florida A & M University, Tallahassee, FL.
1959	October 17 – Blessed to be 20 years old
1960	Attended ROTC Camp in Fort Benning, GA, experienced first close interaction with white people.
1961	June – Graduated from FAMU – political science major, minor in economics
1961	June – Commissioned as an officer in the U.S. Army Reserve.
1961	September – Entered active duty service in the U.S. Army at Ft. Eustis, VA.
1963	August – Departed active military service and enrolled in the Howard University School of Law, Washington, DC.
1966	June – Graduated from Howard Law School – Juris Doctor Degree and accepted a position as a Field Attorney (Law Clerk) with the National Labor Relations Board (NLRB), in its Tampa, Florida Regional Office.

The Journey

1966	Married my one and only wife, Joan Brown Dawson, in her home town of New Bern, NC.
1967	November – Admitted to The Florida Bar.
1967	December – Opened a law office for the private practice law at 3556 N. 29th Street, Tampa FL.
NBA	February – Appointed Assistant City Attorney & City Prosecutor – City of Tampa, FL.
1960s	Charter member - School Biracial Advisory Committee.
1960s	Hillsborough Charter Commission
1969	October 17 – Blessed to be 30 years old
1970	Candidate, Florida House of Representatives, District 64.
1972	Bar Admission – The District of Columbia Bar
1974	Re: Manning v. The School Board – 27 Years
1976	Celebrated the addition of my one and only Daughter, Wendy Hope Dawson
1979	Elected Vice President, National Bar Association.
1979	October 17 – Blessed to be 40 years old
1981	July – Elected President-Elect, National Bar Association at Convention in Detroit, MI
1982	Sworn in as President, National Bar Association at Convention in Atlanta, GA
1983	May – Recognized by Ebony Magazine as one of "The 100 Most Influential Blacks in America"
1988	Appointed to the Committee on The Education of Blacks in Florida.
1989	October 17 – Blessed to be 50 years old
1990	Special Counsel to Hillsborough Board of County Commissioners Re: Ruskin – Wimauma Sewer Construction Litigation
1991	Recipient – "Unsung Hero Award" – Tampa Organization of Black Affairs ("TOBA")
1991	Recipient – "Francisco A. Rodriguez Civil Rights Award" – George Edgecomb Bar Association
1992	Recipient – "Gertrude E. Rush Award" National Bar Association
1992	Recipient – "Distinguished Alumni Award" Florida A & M University
1993	Recipient – "MLK Drum Major for Justice Award" Federal MLK Holiday Commission
1993	Special Counsel to City of Tampa Re: Lykes Bros.,

	Inc. v. City of Tampa Architectural Review Commission
1994	Partner – Dawson and Griffin, P.A. 8/1994 through 3/1996
1995	February 16 – Held Press Conference in support of County Commissioner, Sandra Wilson
1996	Special Bond Counsel to Hillsborough County Aviation Authority
1997	Special Counsel to Tampa General Hospital Re: Tanner v. Tampa General Hospital through 1998
1999	October 17 – Blessed to be 60 years old
2001	Recipient – "Michael A. Fogarty Memorial 'In the Trenches' Award" – Hillsborough County Bar Association
2007	Inductee – National Bar Association Hall of Fame
2009	October 17 – Blessed to be 70 years old
2011	Awarded – "Honorary Doctorate of Humane Letters" by Florida A & M University
2013	Featured in Hillsborough Area Regional Transit Authority ("HART Line") "It All Started on a Bus… with Rosa Parks in 1955." campaign
2014	October 17 – Blessed to be 75 years old
2016	Elected to the Judicial Council of the African Methodist Episcopal Church (AME) at the 200-Year Anniversary of the church in Philadelphia, PA
2017	The Hillsborough County School Board named a new school "Warren Hope Dawson Elementary School" in honor of my 27 years of legal work in the School Desegregation Case known as Manning vs. The School Board. This $20 million educational facility is built to house 900 students in pre-K through the 5th grade.
2017	Inducted as an honorable member of the 100 Black Men of Tampa Bay, Inc.
2017	August 10 – Students' first day ever at the Warren Hope Dawson Elementary School
2018	In April of 2018, the Tampa Bay Lightning recognized my community advocacy with its Community Hero Award. There was a half-time video presentation that covered my career and monetary award of $50,000.00 to the Warren Hope Dawson Elementary School Foundation, Inc - my favorite charity."
2019	October 17 - Blessed to be 80 years old and still practicing law.

Dawson on Dawson

"There much love flowing between individuals such as sister to sister, brother to brother, mother to father, cousin to cousin and friend to friend. But chief among all love is that of mother for her son and a son for his mother. There is no greater love than that."

****

"In my house, Hope became a precedent to expectation. One did not "hope" that something would happen, you were expected to make it happen"

****

"Hope is the light that is within that cannot be extinguished."

****

If some of my so-called friends will promise to stop telling lies about me - I will promise to stop telling the truth about them.

****

Advice: First, find yourself something you can do well, and then the people who want it done will find you.

****

There are some people, who have affected my life in a negative way who were not mentioned in this book. Their omission, by name, is intentional. The primary reasons for that are: (1) They already know who they are; (2) Some of you already know who they are and (3) A few of you don't give-a-dam who they are.

****

There are some friends and others, who have affected my life in positive way who are not mentioned in this book. Their omission, by name, is intentional. The primary reason for that was: I didn't want them to be better known than those mentioned. However, in most instances, they too, already know who they are.

****

You do best what you do most often, and if you don't do it often, you generally don't do it well.

****

As I close, it is important to me that you know the following:

APOSTLES' CREED
(Affirmation of Faith)

I believe in God, the Father Almighty, Maker of heaven and earth, and in Jesus Christ his only Son, our Lord, who was conceived by the Holy Spirit, born of the Virgin Mary, suffered under Pontius Pilate, was crucified, dead, and buried. The third day he arose from the dead; he ascended into heaven, and sits at the right hand of God, the Father Almighty; from thence he shall come to judge the quick and the dead. I believe in the Holy Spirit, the Church Universal, the communion of saints, the forgiveness of sins, the resurrection of the body and the life everlasting. Amen

(As recited in the African Methodist Episcopal Church, the Church of my Faith.)

About The Author

Warren Hope Dawson

Born in Mulberry, Florida, this veteran attorney has fought numerous legal battles to advance civil rights for black people in Tampa Bay, including desegregation of schools and preservation of voting rights.

During his 50-plus year career, Attorney Dawson championed black rights. This Mulberry native is only the third black graduate of a Polk County, Florida public high school to become a lawyer. He was the first black hired in the National Labor Review Board's Tampa regional office and was Tampa's first black assistant city attorney. He helped fight for single-member districts so that minority neighborhoods would have a better chance of being able to elect black candidates.

Perhaps his biggest contribution was serving as lead counsel for the NAACP Legal Defense and Education Fund, Inc. In Manning vs. Hillsborough County School Board, a long-running legal battle that led to the desegregation of Hillsborough County Public Schools.

Prior to the 1990 Super Bowl in Tampa, Dawson pushed for the integration of the then, all - white Ye Mystic Krewe of Gasparilla. He also lobbied against a proposed theme park that would have commercialized a slave ship. Dawson served as the 40th president of the National Bar Association and was inducted into the organization's Hall of Fame, is a life member of The Fellows of the American Bar Association Foundation, and was the national president of the Howard University Law Alumni Association.

In the latest recognition of his contributions, Dawson was elected to the Judicial Council of the African Methodist Episcopal Church, the highest judicatory body of a church estimated to have 7.5 million members in 39 countries.

Attorney Warren Hope Dawson is a local and national treasure.

Index

39th Transportation Battalion 64
Abudulai, Suhuyini 118
ACLU 58
Advisory Board of the
    Tampa Bay Buccaneers 189
Africa, Gabon 197
Africa, Morocco 197
Africa, Rhodesia 159, 160
Africa, Rwanda 197
Africa, Tanzania 197
Africa, Zimbabwe 159, 160, 196
Alabama, Birmingham 65
Alabama, Fort McClellan 65
Alabama, Huntsville 66
Alabama, Macon County 57, 58
Alabama, Phoenix City 68, 69
Alabama, Tuskegee 56, 57
Alexander, Joyce London 153
Almeida, Diana 189
Alpha Phi Alpha Fraternity 189
Ammons, James H 194
Andrews Sr, C. Blythe 110
Andrews, William 191
Anthony, Otis 154
Aquil, Hakin 179
Archer, Dennis 115
Armstead, Ralph 123
Arron, Naomi 208
Askew, Reubin 163
Baltimore 11, 27, 29, 132, 214
Barry, Marion 82, 152
Bell, Edward Frank 162
Ben, Margaret 123
Berlin Crisis 64
Bethune-Cookman College 42
Black, Martin 123
Blair, Ezell 80
Bolden, Victor 127
Borders, Kenneth 51
Bostic, Ashley 207
Bostic, C J 207
Bostic, Clarence 207
Bostic, Wendy 207, 208
Bowers, Theodore 122
Bradley Junction 23
Bradley, Rudolph 177
Brazil, Rio de Janeiro 196
Brown, Benjamin 85
Brown, Wanda 208
Brumick, Henry 170
Bryan, Stuart 192
Bryant, William Vincent 142
Bush, George W. 95, 155
Buster, Dorothy 208
Butler, George Washington 174
California, Los Angeles County 192
California, West Los Angeles 41
Cannon, Darrel 126
Cannon, Nathaniel 126
Cannon, Norman Thomas 126
Cannon, Tyrone 126
Carter, Bubba 39, 40
Carter, Jimmy 186, 191
Chachkin, Norman 127
Chambers, Julius 127
Charles, Cyrus 170
Cherry, Gwendolyn 173
Church, Beulah Baptist 26
AME 70, 71, 73, 74, 75, 76, 80, 81,
    82, 83, 84, 97, 142, 143, 157,
    171, 202, 203, 206, 214, 222
Church, Beulah Baptist 26
Church, First A.M.E 41
Church, Gregg Temple A.M.E. 23
Citrus County 107, 109, 111, 167,
    172
City of Tampa 98, 136, 152, 153,
    169, 176, 215, 216
Clendenen, James 109, 167, 173
Cobb, James W. 162
Cole, Nat King 30, 31, 45
Collins, Robert 122
Conoly, Frank 41
Cooper, Algie 123
Cooper River Bridge 22
Copa Cabana Beach 195
Corbett, C.C. 23

Corbett, J.J. 23
Corbett, Rebecca 23
Crystal River 169
Cuban Missile Crisis 66
Culbreath, H.L. 192
Culbreath, Hugh 192
Culbreath, John R. 108, 192
Culverhouse, Hugh 192
Cunningham, Thomas James "T.J." 162
Danzey, Alexis 208
Danzey, Jessica 208
Danzey, Nina 208
Davis, Al 176
Davis, Marva 123
Davis, Sam 192
Davis, Sammy 23
Dawson, Adam Lee 17
Dawson, Japhus Lloyd 17, 33, 36, 50, 214
Dawson, Crista 208
Dawson (Hurst), Margaret 35
Dawson, James Raymond 35
Dawson, Japhus Lloyd 17, 33, 36, 50, 214
Dawson, Joan Brown 206, 208, 215
Dawson, Margaret 35
Dawson, Naomi Warren 17, 20, 97, 214
Dawson, Patricia 201
Dawson, Wendy Hope 207, 215
DC, Washington 70, 74, 77, 78, 80, 81, 82, 84, 109, 115, 141, 142, 143, 152, 202, 206, 214
de Klerk, F. W. 159
Diecidue, Dennis 189
Dixon, Dud 148
Dorsett, Mary Alice 191
Dozier Reform School 37
Dupree, J. D. 26
Eckstine, Billy 30, 45
Edgecomb, George E. 171
Edwards, Christal 118
Egypt 197
Egypt, Cairo 197
Elder Michaux 26

FAMU 25, 47, 51, 54, 59, 60, 70, 71, 73, 74, 75, 76, 80, 81, 82, 83, 84, 94, 97, 142, 143, 156, 157, 171, 201, 202, 203, 206, 214, 215, 216, 222
Father Devine 26
Favata, Angelo Frank 169
Ferguson, Wilkie 123
Fessor Murray 40
Filipovich, Rosemary 202
Fleet Banks 195
Florida, Agricola 26
Florida, Bartow 27, 30, 43, 44, 45, 48, 73, 77, 93, 138, 139, 148, 214
Florida, Brewster 48
Florida, Brooksville 169
Florida, Clearwater 26
Florida, Dade City 139, 143, 169
Florida, Fort Meade 42, 48
Florida, Fullers Heights 48
Florida, Gordonville 48
Florida, Hernando County 107, 109, 111, 167, 172
Florida, Hillsborough County 11, 12, 99, 106, 107, 108, 109, 125, 127, 128, 133, 150, 153, 163, 167, 168, 169, 170, 171, 172, 176, 178, 187, 191, 216, 222
Florida, Homeland 48
Florida, Jacksonville 192
Florida, Lakeland 29, 32, 36, 40, 55, 76, 138, 144, 148
Florida Legislature 98, 166, 174, 183
Florida, Manatee County 167, 177
Florida, Medulla 144
Florida, Mulberry 12, 15, 17, 19, 22, 26, 27, 29, 35, 36, 37, 40, 44, 46, 48, 55, 73, 77, 105, 144, 148, 156, 160, 165, 175, 177, 192, 196, 214, 221, 222
Florida, New Port Richey 169
Florida, Nichols 48
Florida, Pasco County 107, 109, 111, 137, 139, 167, 172
Florida, Plant City 169, 177
Florida, Polk County 19, 43, 50, 97, 138,

146, 147, 149, 222
Florida, Prairie 12, 17, 19, 21
Florida Probation & Parole Qualifications Committee 189
Florida, Progress Village 169
Florida Sentinel 93, 198
Florida Sentinel Bulletin 93, 97, 198
Florida, Springhill 169
Florida, St. Petersburg 60, 170, 173, 174, 192
Florida, Swift 26
Florida, Tampa 3, 11, 17, 21, 27, 80, 81, 84, 85, 93, 96, 97, 98, 99, 102, 103, 106, 108, 109, 116, 130, 131, 136, 137, 139, 150, 151, 152, 153, 154, 156, 163, 165, 167, 169, 170, 173, 176, 177, 180, 187, 189, 192, 196, 198, 201, 202, 203, 214, 215, 216, 221, 222
Florida, Temple Terrace 169
Florida, Wauchula 192
Florida, West Palm Beach 40
Flowers, Katrena 208
Fluker, Betty 60
Ford Foundation 74
Foster, William Patrick 94
Franklin, Elmer 37, 38
Frank, Pat 169
Freedman, Sandy 154, 155
Fuller, R. B. 19, 50
Gage, George 192
Gallaudet University 82
Gasparilla 150, 151, 152, 153, 178, 196, 222
Gaulman, Saundra 208
General Telephone & Electric (GTE) Telephone Company 192
Georgia, Atlanta 85, 131, 215
Georgia, Columbus 70
Georgia, Fort Benning 56, 57, 59, 64, 66, 67, 69, 70, 73
Georgia, Savannah 56, 85, 150
Gibbons, Sam 84
Glover, Jessie 208
Graham, Julian N 172

Gray, Fred D 162
Greco, Angelo L 172
Greco, Dick 97, 172
Gregg, John Andrew 23
Gregory, Rodney 122
Grinan, Sylvia 191
Hammond, James A 154, 191
Hargrett, James 166, 174, 175, 177, 178
Harris, Patricia Roberts 202
Harvey, Jerry N 191
Harvey, Perry 110, 143, 191, 198
Hatch, Orrin 109, 110
Hatter, Debra 118
HCC 201
Hicks, Ron 193
Hill, Bobby 80, 85
Hill, Horace 123
Hinson, Altamese 41
Holifield, Bishop 122
Holland, Spessard L 73, 77, 78, 139
Hollowell, Donald Lee 162
Holyfield, Marilyn 118, 203
House, Carolyn 123
Houston, Charles Hamilton 81
Hunter, Henry 123
Hurst, Celest 208
Hutchinson, William 123
Hyde, Gilbert 169
IMC 19, 21, 48, 49, 50
Jackson, Jesse 121
Jamaica, Kingston 161
Jenkins, Doris 122
Jennings, J Blayne 123
Johnson, William 123
Jones, Arthur 154, 162
Jones, B. Margretta 24
Jones, Charles 76
Jones, Elaine 126, 127, 202, 203
Jones, John Arthur 162
Kansas, Topeka 125
Kelly, Richard 122, 139, 140, 141, 142, 143
Kelly, Walter 122
Kennedy, Bobby 76

Kennedy, Jane 214
Kennedy, John F. 76, 82
Kenyatta, Jomo 162
Kershaw, Joe Lang 173
Knight, Gladys 13
Knopke, Ray C. 166, 172
Knowles, Harold 123
Knox, George F. 102
Kovachevich, Elizabeth A. 203
Krentzman, Ben 128
Kynes, James 162
Kynes, James "Jimmy" 192
Lake, Paul 192
Lane, Thomas A. 169
Latimer, Henry 122
Lawson, Marjorie 202
Lee, John Robert Edward 47
Lee Jr, J.R.E. 40, 47
Linder, Scott 193
Little, Perry 123
llinois, Chicago 27
Louisiana, New Orleans 129, 150, 196
Lowrey, Bob 193
Mahan, Johnny 123
Mandela, Nelson 158, 159, 196
Manning 12, 126, 127, 128, 132, 133, 203, 215, 216, 222
Manning, Andrew L. 126
Manning, Willie M. 126
Mark, Bill 43
Marks, John 123
Marshall, Reese 123
Marshall, Thurgood 81, 90, 127, 203
Martin, Sadie 177
Martin, Tommie 21
Maryland, Baltimore 11, 27, 29, 132, 214
Mass, Boston 153, 195
McAllister, Julius Harrison 200
McCelland, William R 189
McCoy Air Force Base 66
McDonald, Gabrielle Kirk 203
McEwen, James M. "Red" 192

McEwen, Red 192
McEwen, Tom 192
McKennie, Forrest 93
McLean, Jack 122
Memphis Army Depot 66, 67
Michican, Detroit 113, 215
Miller, Leslie 174
Miller, Thomas A. 169
Milton, Morris 122, 173, 174
Miss Precious 40
Mondale, Walter F. 120
Monroe, Cordelia 27
Montgomery, James D 214
Montour, Sheryl 118
Moore, Cecil 157, 158
Morrell, Joseph 122
Morrison, Robert 123
Motley, Constance Baker 127, 203
Motley, Frank 118
Motter, Anna 122
Mugabe, Robert 159, 160, 161, 196
Murray, "Fessor" E. W. 40
Myers, Randolph 126
Myers, Renee 126
NAACP 80, 127, 130, 132, 173, 203
Naomi Warren Dawson 17, 20, 214
National Bar Association 84, 111, 115, 118, 120, 121, 157, 158, 161, 178, 203, 215, 216, 222
National Labor Review Board 222
Nelson, Horace 56
New England Conservatory Orchestra 195
NLRB 80, 109, 111, 167, 202, 214
North Carolina, Greensboro 80
North Carolina, New Bern 84, 206, 215
Nunn, Isaac 122
Orlando 11, 66, 99
Orlando International Airport 66
Otudeko, Bernice 208
Parks, Jeanus 162
Pennsylvania, Philadelphia 24, 157, 158, 216
Pepin, Art 192
Perry, Matthew 162

Phillips, Lloyd 193
Pope, Dick 193
Porter, Ann 126
Powell Jr, Adam Clayton 82, 83
Powell vs. McCormack 84
Project Pride 98
Prophet Jones 26
Purdy, Monica McCoy 208
Randolph, Roosevelt 122
Ransom, James 154
Reagan, Ronald 116
Reddick, Thomas J. 163
Reed, Betty 166, 179, 181
Reed, Sandra B. 126
Reeves, Frank 82
Regan, Ronald 186, 188
Reid, Herbert O. 83
Richardson, Jonathan 118
Richardson Jr, Adam Jefferson 200
Rivers, Alline 208
Rodriguez, Francisco 126, 132, 162
Rogers, Eddie 122
Rogers-LaFontant, Jewel Stradford 157
Rolle, Leon 123
Ross, Steve 169
ROTC 54, 56, 59
Roundtree, Dovey 202
Sanderlin, James 132, 170
Sanders, Nathaniel 126, 144, 145, 146, 148, 149, 150
Saunders, Robert 126
School, Blake High 128
School, Marshall High 128
School, Middleton High 128
School, Pinellas High 93
School, Roosevelt High 40
School, Union Academy High 30, 45, 46, 48, 93, 214
School, Washington Park High 40
Scionti, Mike 169
Scruggs, Frank 122
Shear, David 162
Simmons, Malvis 42
Simmons, Willie Lawrence 42

Smith, H.T. 123
Smith, Ian 160
Smith, Luther 122
Smith, Roosevelt 38
Smith, William Reece 97, 132, 136
South Africa, Pretoria 196
South Africa, Zimbabwe 159, 160, 196
South Carolina, Anderson 22, 32, 35, 36, 138
South Carolina, Darlington 21, 22, 24, 34, 36, 37
South Carolina, Florence 78, 80
Stephens, James 45
Stevens, Thomas A. 108
Stevens, William 122
St. Petersburg Times 192
Stringer, Thomas 122, 189
Super Bowl 150, 151, 152, 178, 222
Sweet Daddy Grace 26
Swift, Agricola 26
Tampa Bay Buccaneers 189, 192
Tampa, Belmont Heights 169
Tampa Bulletin 93
Tampa Electric (TECO) 192
Tampa, Progress Village 169
Tampa Red Cross Board 189
Tampa Tribune Newspaper 109, 173, 192
Tampa Urban League Board 189
Taylor, Carol 203
Tennessee, Memphis 66, 67, 155
The Bigger Digger 49
Thompson, Bobby 102, 136
Thompson, Dudley 161
Thompson, Emerson 123
Tilly The Toiler 49
Timberlake Federal Building 81, 106
TOBA 106, 215
Tokley, Joanna 154
Travis, Robert 122
Tyus, Willie 59
Union Foreign Missionary Baptist Association, INC. 26
University Club 152, 153

University, Florida A & M 25, 215, 216
University, Florida State 54
University, Howard 70, 71, 73, 74, 75,
    76, 80, 81, 82, 83, 84, 97, 142,
    143, 157, 171, 202, 203, 206,
    214, 222
University, North Carolina A&T 80
U.S. Department of Justice National
    Advisory Board 189
Virginia, Arlington County 84, 206
Virginia, Fort Eustis 64
Virginia, Norfolk 27
Vizcaino, Victor 189
Walker, Joseph 170
Walker, Shirley 122
Warren, Adam 16, 17, 34, 82, 83, 214
Warren, Carl 176
Warren, Letha 16, 17, 34, 82, 83, 214
Warren, Willie 176
Washington, Alfred 122
Washington, Harold 116
Washington, Seattle 116, 118
Washington, Walter 82
Watts, Danny 123
Weeks, Renee 214
Wells, Orzo Thaddeus "OT" 162
Wesley, Eugene 37, 38, 76
Wesley, Jeanette 51
Wesley, Ruby 51
West Tampa 169
West, W. D. (Doug) 169
Wheaton, Freida L. 118
White, Bobby Gene 76
White, John Franklin 200
White, Larry 122
Whydah Galley 153, 154, 155, 156
Williams, Isaac 122
Williams, Lorenzo 162
Williams, Rickie 123
Williams, Ricky 176
Williams, Vernice 17
Will Mastin Trio 23
Wilson, Charles 162
Wright, Kaydell 203
Wright, Zebedee 123

Ye Mystic Krewe 150, 151, 153, 222